Dalmatian

◇

By Frances Camp

Contents

Training Your Dalmatian 80

By Charlotte Schwartz
Be informed about the importance of training your Dalmatian from the basics of housebreaking and understanding the development of a young dog to executing obedience commands (sit, stay, down, etc.).

Health Care of Your Dalmatian 104

Discover how to select a qualified vet and care for your dog at all stages of life. Topics include vaccinations, skin problems, dealing with external and internal parasites and common medical and behavioral conditions.

Your Senior Dalmatian 138

Recognize the signs of an aging dog, both behavioral and medical; implement a senior-care program with your veterinarian and become comfortable with making the final decisions and arrangements for your senior Dalmatian.

Showing Your Dalmatian 147

Enter the dog show world and find out how dog shows work and how a champion is made. Go beyond the conformation ring to different types of trials and performance events.

KENNEL CLUB BOOKS: **DALMATIAN**
ISBN: 1-59378-225-X

Copyright © 1999 • Revised American Edition: Copyright © 2003
Kennel Club Books, Inc., 308 Main Street, Allenhurst, NJ 07711 USA
Cover Design Patented: US 6,435,559 B2 • Printed in South Korea

Photographs by:
Norvia Behling, T. J. Calhoun, Carolina Biological Supply, Doskocil, Isabelle Français, James Hayden-Yoav, James R. Hayden, RBP, Carol Ann Johnson, Dwight R. Kuhn, Dr. Dennis Kunkel, Mikki Pet Products, Antonio Philippe, Phototake, Jennifer Porbansky, Jean Claude Revy, Dr. Andrew Spielman, Alice van Kempen and C. James Webb.

Illustrations by Renée Low.

HISTORY OF THE

DALMATIAN

ANCIENT BEGINNINGS

Although it is known that the Dalmatian is a very old breed, its exact origins are somewhat of a mystery. Evidence of Dalmatian-like dogs can be found in artifacts from civilizations as old as ancient Egypt, as drawings of spotted dogs have been found on cave walls and in Egyptian tombs. These early drawings depict the dogs running beside chariots pulled by horses. Some historians maintain that ancient Egypt is, in fact, the birthplace of the Dalmatian breed.

There are also those who believe that the region formerly known as Yugoslavia is where the Dalmatian's roots lie and that a man named Jurij Dalmatin is the originator of the breed. There is evidence that Dalmatin had received dogs from Turkey and bred them in the latter part of the sixteenth century. The dogs became known as "Dalmatins" or "Turkish Dogs," but there is no written description of what these dogs looked like. To add to the confusion, there is a province on the Adriatic Sea called Dalmatia,

a name that often causes people to believe that it is the Dalmatian's homeland (though there is no evidence to support this assumption).

One thing that is constant about the Dalmatian's history is their association with horses. From the ancient cave drawing to seventeenth- and eighteenth-century artwork depicting spotted dogs, the dogs are almost always pictured with horses. Along with the dogs' striking markings, it is their affinity for horses that caused the dogs to be prized by traveling

Opposite page: Although the exact origin of the Dalmatian is still uncertain, today it is one of the most distinct-looking and recognizable breeds in the world.

The harlequin Great Dane has been suggested as one of the Dalmatian's ancestors. Judging from looks, this theory is quite probable.

Harlequin Great Dane puppies bear an amazing similarity to Dalmatian puppies.

Romany gypsies. This is yet another factor that adds to the cloudiness of the Dalmatian's origin. These spotted dogs were "spotted" all over Europe, most likely introduced into many different regions through their travels. Thus, it is difficult to ascertain where the dogs were first found.

THE DALMATIAN GOES TO ENGLAND

Once the Dalmatian reached England, the breed's history becomes easier to trace. The breed is a very old one in England, tracing back to around the late seventeenth century. The Dalmatian first gained popularity among the upper class in England, where the dogs were used as coach dogs for both protective and ornamental purposes. Dalmatians were used to guard their masters' horses and coaches while traveling. The Dalmatian would run with the coach, either behind the horses' heels or underneath one of the coach's axles. When the passengers had to make a stop and leave the coach unattended, the Dalmatian would guard the horses, the coach and the coach's contents. During overnight stops, the Dalmatian would stay in the stable with the horses and coach to ward off thieves.

The Dalmatian became very well known as the "coach dog," and was prized for his tireless ability to keep pace on long journeys. Add to this the dog's uncanny sense of kinship with the horses, and it seemed that coaching was indeed the Dalmatian's purpose; no other breed was better suited to the task. The Dalmatian, with his distinctive spots, was already an easily recognizable breed to begin with, but now he was also an almost permanent fixture beside coaches all over England. Unfortunately, when the use of automobiles became commonplace and the use of the horse-drawn carriage eventually was phased out, the Dalmatian was no longer needed to perform what had

UK BREED CLUBS

In the UK, there are four major Dalmatian breed clubs:
- The North of England Dalmatian Club (NEDC), founded in 1903
- The British Dalmatian Club (BDC), founded in 1925 as the Southern Dalmatian Club
- The Dalmatian Club of Scotland (DCS), founded in 1969
- The Northern Ireland Dalmatian Club (NIDC), founded in 1981

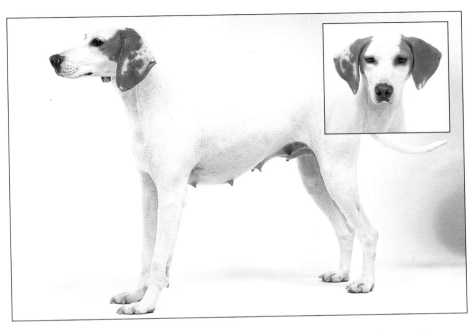

The smooth Istrian Pointer, probably from the former Yugoslavia, is also among the Dalmatian's ancestors.

Inset: Head study of the Istrian Pointer.

become his intended duty.

Dals also gained their fame as "firehouse dogs" in Britain. The dogs were kept by London firemen to rid the firehouses of rats and similar pests, but because of the dogs' love of horses and instinct for coaching, they would often run along with the horse-drawn fire wagons. One could often witness a Dalmatian running in front of a fire wagon, as if to blaze a trail and clear the path for the firemen. With the advent of motorized fire trucks came a change for the Dalmatian as well—he then became a passenger in the truck, seated next to the driver. Although it is rare today to

FIRST UK SPECIALTIES

The first specialty shows of both the North of England Dalmatian Club and the Southern Dalmatian Club were held in the same year, 1930. The Southern Dalmatian Club also changed its name in 1930 to the British Dalmatian Club, the name by which the club is known today.

The Bengal Harrier, as shown in this illustration from the 1700s, seems like a sure bet to have been the Dalmatian's predecessor. Early English dog books credit the Old English hounds as the origin of the Dalmatian.

CRUFTS CHAMP
In 1968 a Dalmatian, Eng. Ch. Fanhill Faune, was the Supreme Champion at Crufts Dog Show, the UK's largest and most prestigious dog show.

see a Dalmatian accompanying a fire company to fight a fire, the distinction of "firehouse dog" has remained with the breed.

The Dalmatian's popularity in England was not just as a coaching

Above: Eng. Ch. Golden Dawn of Coelan is a beautiful bitch from the 1930s with good markings. Owned by Miss Stephenson. Right: In a photo from 1931, the beautiful Miss Griselda Hervey poses with her two pet Dalmatians.

was able to provide breeding stock after the war.

While Dalmatians were popular before the war, their popularity really blossomed after the war. In 1918, there were two Kennel-Club-registered Dalmatians. Then, in a span of less than 15 years, registrations skyrocketed to nearly 900! It

Look at that! This Dalmatian is as alert as his young friend as an airplane passes overhead in this photo from the early 1930s.

Miss L. B. Clay was a famous English exhibitor of Dalmatians and well known at the UK's Crufts show. One of her pups is pictured here, just when he was starting to get his spots.

dog and a firehouse mascot. The dogs also became popular in the show ring. Britain's second conformation show was held in 1860, and this is the first time that Dalmatians were shown. The first breed standard, which was The Kennel Club's first official standard for the breed, was published in 1890. However, for about the next 30 years, there were very few records of Dalmatian champions. In 1925 the Southern Dalmatian Club (now the British Dalmatian Club) was formed, with Mr. Fred Kemp as president. Mr. Kemp is a major reason that there were any Dalmatians left in England at that time, as he kept the Dals in his kennel alive through the devastation of World War I and, as a result,

ROAD TRIALS

A major effort on the part of the Dalmatian Club of America to preserve the Dalmatian's original function was the introduction of road trial competition. The first road trial was held in Pennsylvania in 1906. Each dog ran with a horse and carriage and the dogs were scored: 75% on coaching ability and 25% on conformation. Toward the middle of the century, the carriages were eliminated and each dog ran with a rider on horseback, covering distances of either 12.5 or 25 miles. The DCA still sponsors road trials, usually in conjunction with its national specialties if held in an appropriate location.

101 DALMATIANS

In 1956, English author Dodie Smith's *101 Dalmatians* was published (yes, it originated as a book!). The animated Disney movie *101 Dalmatians* followed in 1961, and 1996 saw the Disney re-release of the movie, this time with live people and dogs!

and show dog has remained relatively constant. Dalmatian breed clubs in the UK are committed to preserving the Dalmatian and disseminating information about the breed to prospective owners. Today the Dalmatian ranks among the top 20 most popular breeds in the UK, according to the number of Kennel Club registrations.

A lovely group of Dalmatian pups. Their spotting is still at an early stage in this photo.

was during this time period that many important bloodlines were established in England. These quality dogs improved the breed all over the world, as many English-born Dalmatians of this time, or their offspring, were exported to other countries and became foundation stock. An example is the "of the Wells" strain; this line not only produced top winners in England but many "of the Wells" dogs also figured prominently in the foundations of important American kennels.

Since the end of World War II, the Dalmatian's popularity as a pet

THE DALMATIAN IN THE UNITED STATES

The Dalmatian is quite a star in the United States, thanks in no small part to Disney and the *101 Dalmatians* movies (and what seems to be the requisite marketing and merchandise blitz). It took them some time to gain their popularity in the US, but it wasn't too long before Americans were "seeing spots" everywhere. Top-quality English bloodlines have much to do with the improvement of the Dalmatian in the USA. While records show that George Washington owned "coach dogs"

Champion Dalmatians from the 1930s, all belonging to the well-known breeder Mrs. D. K. Hackney. Ch. Snow Leopard, second from the right, was world-famous during his career.

as early as the late eighteenth century, the first Dalmatian was not registered with the American Kennel Club until 1887—this was a bitch named "Bessie."

The first record of a Dalmatian in conformation competition in America was in 1883, but the breed was not particularly popular. The first Dalmatian champion was recorded in 1904; this is also the year in which the organizational foundation was being laid down for the Dalmatian Club of America (DCA). The DCA was officially founded in 1905, and the formation of a breed club did

much to increase the Dalmatian's popularity in the US.

Registration was not required in the early days of conformation showing, so registrations alone are not the most accurate way to determine the number of Dalmatians. The northeastern United States was where the Dalmatian first gained popularity; this is where much of the showing activity took place. Dalmatians were shown not only in conformation competition but also in road-trial competition, which became very popular. These were tests that evaluated the dogs' natural

DCA ONLINE
The Dalmatian Club of America has a wonderful web site (www.thedca.org), which can help you find a breeder and puppy, update you on the latest health advances, put you in touch with breed clubs and rescue organizations in your area, tell you about upcoming Dal events, and the list goes on!

Miss Barnes' top-winning bitch Westella Venture shows the breed's beautiful head.

Mother and pups make a pretty picture. Note the difference in the spotting pattern on the ears of each dog.

aptitude for coaching, the purpose for which the breed was intended. Conformation played a small part in these tests, but the focus was on the dogs' working ability.

American Dals also became "firehouse dogs" just like their English counterparts; they were highly valued by the firemen as companions. When the company was called to the scene of a fire, the Dalmatian often appointed himself an "honorary firefighter" and came along on foot. Today many fire companies adopt Dalmatians as mascots. Dalmatians are often used in demonstrations to give fire safety lessons to schoolchildren. It is very common to see Dalmatian

collectibles and trinkets depicting the dogs wearing fire hats or in fire trucks. "Fire engine red" is a color very often associated with the Dalmatian; many owners "dress" their Dals in red collars, believing that red is the color in which their dogs look best!

Dalmatians are very popular today in the US, with a large pet population and consistently large entries in specialty and all-breed shows. Dalmatians participate in a wide range of activities in America, including agility and obedience trials, road trial competition, flyball, hiking, backpacking and much more. The Dalmatian is also used as a therapy dog and as an assistance dog. Because of the huge demand for Dalmatian puppies created by the re-creation of Disney's *101 Dalmatians*, the DCA has done much to promote responsible breeding, responsible ownership and Dalmatian rescue.

rest of the world may not think of the Dalmatian in this capacity (he is part of the AKC's Non-Sporting Group), the Dalmatian became as much of a sporting dog as any of the retrievers, spaniels or setters.

The first records of Dalmatians in conformation competition were

Although not typically thought of as a retrieving breed, the Dalmatian is prized for his abilities as a water retriever.

THE DALMATIAN IN AUSTRALIA

The Dalmatian has found a wonderful home in Australia. Its purpose here was a bit different than in England or the US— although the Dal did accompany their masters traveling on horseback, he was used mainly as a hunter and water retriever. Owners were amazed at how well these dogs took to water and, while the

in the late 1880s, but the breed did not do anything significant in the show ring until the 1930s. The '30s and '40s were important decades for the Dalmatian in Australia, as this is when the breed gained recognition and much of the foundation stock was established. With the importation of English, and sometimes American, stock and the subsequent rise in the breed's quality and popularity

A modern example of a beautiful Dalmatian bred in the Netherlands.

came the Dalmatian's first real strides in the show ring.

Today there are many outstanding Australian Dalmatian bloodlines, and dogs continue to be imported as well. The Dalmatian is very popular in Australia and very well known for his versatility. He is seen in numerous areas of the dog sport, including conformation, obedience, agility, endurance testing, flyball and tracking. Rules for dog competition in Australia are set forth by the governing councils in each Australian state and by the Australian National Kennel Council (ANKC), which is made up of these councils.

Of course, the Dalmatian is a popular choice for a companion dog, and he is gaining fame as a performer (as is the case in much of the world). He finds a special place in firehouses throughout Australia and has been featured in numerous public safety programs, on fire safety and other topics, geared toward children.

Dalmatians in training at a kennel in the 1920s. This looks like the precursor to modern agility training!

THE DALMATIAN IN GERMANY

In Germany the Dalmatian is well over 300 years old, and just like their English counterparts, it took German Dalmatians quite some time before they attracted much attention. Two Dalmatians were entered in a show in 1879, and for the next few decades entries rose slowly but consistently. World War I, of course, had a detrimental effect on the breed, and the first Dalmatian breed club (*Deutscher Dalmatiner Club von 1920 e.V.*) in Germany was formed several years later in an attempt to revive breeding activity and improve quality. In the years between the two World Wars, breed clubs began to fall under very strict regulation. During the wars, there was virtually no breeding of dogs of any breed. Once breeding resumed after World War II, more conflict ensued with the split of the country into East and West Germany.

Breeding began again following the division, but Dalmatian breeders in East Germany and West Germany may as well have been breeding two separate breeds. The Dalmatians resembled each other in looks, but were on opposite ends of the spectrum in terms of personality. West German breeders bred mild-tempered companion dogs, while East German breeders bred slightly aggressive dogs designed for protection work. Since the reunification of Germany, breeders across the country have united and major breed clubs have joined together for the purpose of solidifying type and temperament in the Dalmatian. Also, there has been an increase in imports since 1989, which has done much to contribute to the quality of the German Dalmatian bloodlines. The *Deutscher Dalmatiner Club von 1920 e.V.* still exists and operates today under the Fédération Cynologique Internationale (FCI), the ruling organization for dog activity in continental Europe.

WORLDWIDE POPULARITY

Dalmatians are popular worldwide, with much foundation stock coming from English, American and German bloodlines. From Canada to South Africa and almost everywhere in between, national breed clubs are dedicated to

preserving and promoting the Dalmatian. No matter where in the world the Dalmatian is "spotted," there is no doubt that he is one of the most distinctive-looking dog breeds of all time, and perhaps the most recognizable. Breed fanciers around the globe today strive to let the world know that the Dalmatian has more than just his unique look—behind those spots lies a wonderfully rich and ancient heritage.

Top: Ch. Midstone Ebony, owned by Mrs. J. W. Bonney, was bred in England and exported to the USA. Bottom: Goworth Victor, owned by Miss E. V. Barnes, was an English-bred Dalmatian and a Crufts winner.

CHARACTERISTICS OF THE

DALMATIAN

The answer to the question, "Why the Dalmatian?" is, on the surface, a very easy one. Why? Because those spots are something else! Why? Because they have such exuberant, outgoing personalities. Why? Because we just saw *101 Dalmatians* and want a dog just like Pongo or Perdita.

True, the Dalmatian is a beautiful, distinctive-looking dog with a wonderfully gregarious personality. However, if your impressions of what the breed is all about are based on what you've seen in a movie, then you have a lot more learning to do. If you're bowled over by the thought of bringing an adorable spotted puppy home, it's time to look

Dalmatians make wonderful pets provided that they have enough attention and activity. They want nothing more than to be part of the family!

beyond the spots. In order to be a responsible and informed dog owner, and this goes for dogs of any breed, it is not sufficient to decide to add a dog to your family simply because you saw one on TV and it "looked cute." Dogs are dogs and, in reality, the pup you bring home will not behave like the highly trained animals used in TV and movies. All of this is being said not to dissuade the potential Dalmatian owner, because they are indeed wonderful dogs. Wonderful dogs, yes. The perfect dog for everyone, no. This information is being presented to give the prospective owner important facts about the Dalmatian. So read on, and if the Dalmatian is in fact the breed for you, may you enjoy a long and fulfilling life with your new spotted friend.

Even at a young age, the breed's elegance is evident in this beautiful pup from Dutch breeding.

PHYSICAL CHARACTERISTICS

Let's start off with the obvious. The Dalmatian is one of the world's most recognizable dog breeds and the reason is obvious…the spots, of course. From a purely esthetic point of view, the spots are what make the Dalmatian a Dalmatian. While the spots are the Dalmatian's "beauty marks," they are far from being the breed's most important physical trait when it comes to soundness.

The Dalmatian is a medium-sized dog with an athletic-looking body. A Dalmatian in good condition is an awesome sight with sleek, clean lines. Remember that the Dalmatian was a working breed by design, and the fact that the breed is no longer used in that capacity is no excuse for obese, out-of-shape dogs. Although most Dals would run all day if they had the choice, regular, not excessive, exercise is all that is needed to keep a healthy Dalmatian looking fit.

Overall, the Dalmatian

NICKNAMES

Throughout history, the Dalmatian's trademark spots have earned him some interesting nicknames like "Plum Pudding Dog" and "Spotted Dick."

The Dalmatian is a medium-sized dog with a muscular, athletic-looking body. He requires training and exercise to make him the ideal pet.

should be balanced and well proportioned. It should not be exaggerated in any one feature. These are essential characteristics of a dog that needs to use energy efficiently for maximum endurance.

The Dalmatian is not a long-coated breed (although long-haired Dals are known to exist), but the length of the coat varies from dog to dog. The coat should be smooth and, while the Dalmatian does not require an elaborate grooming routine, the prospective owner should know that Dalmatians shed! White hairs on your black sweater, black hairs on your white sofa…of course, this is a small inconvenience compared to the joy your pet Dalmatian will bring to you, but something to consider nonetheless.

These little puppies will eventually have large spots like Mom. The breed has a very unique look thanks to its spots.

The shedding can be kept to a minimum easily with regular brushing to remove dead hair.

Along with an exuberant dog comes an exuberant tail…so watch your breakables! You'll be amazed at how quickly a Dal can clear a table with an enthusiastically wagging tail. Take precautions ahead of time and keep everything out of reach.

PERSONALITY
Exuberance, energy and affection… these are all appropriate words with which to describe the Dalmatian. This is a breed with a real zest for life, and he enjoys being involved in all types of activities. He is intelligent and highly trainable, though stubborn at times, and can learn to do almost anything…and do it well. The most important thing, though, is that he is involved in activities

with his owner. Of course, any Dal will welcome the opportunity to run off some of his energy in the yard, but he will much prefer having a playmate. A run, a walk, a game of frisbee…the Dalmatian loves to do all sorts of things and he especially enjoys when these activities are time spent with his owner as well.

The Dalmatian's love of people may sound surprising, considering that the breed originated as a working dog and, due to the nature of his duties, developed an air of independence. This independent attitude can surface sometimes in the Dal's tendency to "explore" if left unsupervised. While Dalmatians at times may seem to

have minds of their own, they are, in fact, very people-oriented. The Dalmatian has a strong loyalty to and affection for people, especially his owners.

Remember that even though the Dal's coaching duties made him somewhat independent because he had to be trusted to do his job without constant instruction from his master, he still grew accustomed to accompanying his master everywhere. Couple the breed's love of people with its intelligence, and you'll find that Dals are extremely in tune to people's moods. It seems as if they understand how their owners are feeling and can modify

Generally speaking, Dalmatians are full of energy and exuberance… but every dog needs to rest now and then.

One of the pleasures of owning a well-bred and well-trained dog is the fun of showing him and winning prizes.

their behavior accordingly. If you're ready to play, the Dalmatian will follow suit happily. On the other hand, if something is troubling you, the Dal will be just as happy to curl up next to you and commiserate.

Some common misconceptions about Dalmatians are that they are hyper and generally hard to control. Well, this can be said about any dog of any breed without discipline and training—it just happens to be more evident in particularly active breeds. True, Dalmatians are energetic dogs and they need activity, so anyone considering owning a Dalmatian should be prepared for that. This is an inherent characteristic of the breed, and owners should not expect that a Dal will adapt happily to being confined in a small place with no room to run. Training should start at an early age and be strictly enforced. A naturally high-energy dog with no discipline makes a most undesirable combination, so it is no surprise that an untrained Dalmatian could give one a negative impression of the breed.

The Dalmatian is not the kind of dog that should be left outside

"Why don't you have spots, too?" The ever-curious Dalmatian introduces himself to a baby lamb.

all day. As much as the Dal loves his exercise, he loves equally his time in the house as part of the family. He wants to be involved in what's going on with his family, whether it be an evening in front of the television or the hustle and bustle of preparing for the day. He makes a good pet for families with children, provided that the children are educated as to how to treat a dog properly. A child's energy level is a good match for that of the Dalmatian.

It is also often thought that the Dal tends to be a bit dog-aggressive. Again, this is a function of his original purpose as protector of horses and coach. If a stray dog approached, it was the Dalmatian's duty to ward him off. Dog aggression is easily avoided in the pet Dalmatian with early and consistent socialization. The Dal's natural guarding instinct, though, can be an asset in a pet household, as you can count on him to bark a warning if something is amiss!

OWNER SUITABILITY
The best type of owner for a Dalmatian is one who has ample time and patience to care for a dog. This is not a breed to be left

Dalmatians have a long history of being associated with fire-fighters, especially during the times when fire-fighting equipment was drawn by horses.

in the yard unattended, but free play is a wonderful outlet for the Dalmatian's energy under proper supervision. There are Dalmatians who are kept in smaller homes and apartments, but the responsibility then falls on the owner to take the dog elsewhere for exercise.

Dalmatians can thrive in most types of environments. Dals in warm climates often enjoy hiking, backpacking and walks on the beach, while Dals in colder regions have fun romping in the snow. Whatever the climate, the Dalmatian needs balance between outdoor activity and spending time indoors with the family.

to its own devices. The Dalmatian has the kind of personality that can be wonderful if molded into appropriate behavior, but can be a lot to handle if the dog is not taught how to behave.

Another positive quality in a Dalmatian owner is someone who is naturally active and who enjoys participating in a variety of things. The Dalmatian is happiest when involved in something with his owner, so if someone who is already active is able to incorporate his Dalmatian into his activities, it provides a natural and mutual bond between dog and owner.

A Dalmatian is best kept in a house with a sufficiently sized, securely fenced yard. It is never advised to let a Dalmatian run free

BREED-SPECIFIC HEALTH CONSIDERATIONS

Some health problems that affect the Dalmatian are briefly discussed here, not to dissuade a prospective owner or to alarm a new owner, but rather to present helpful information. All Dalmatian owners and anyone who is considering owning a Dalmatian should be aware of this information in order to keep their Dals problem-free.

Deafness is a condition often associated with the Dalmatian. Although it is not a *health* problem in the sense that it makes the dog sick or compromises its lifespan if otherwise healthy, it is a problem nonetheless. A Dalmatian is either born with the ability to hear or it is not; it is not something he can "catch" as he grows up. The best preventative is to buy a puppy from a reputable breeder who can show you documented proof that the pup and its parents have undergone BAER (Brainstem Auditory Evoked Response) testing and have tested as having normal hearing.

Urinary tract infections and stones are another problem in Dalmatians, but not all dogs are affected. With the proper preventatives, even dogs who have the tendency to form stones can live their entire lives stone-free.

Most Dalmatians truly love their masters and will follow them wherever they go.

Discuss preventative measures with your breeder and vet.

Dalmatians have sensitive skin and are prone to allergies and other irritants that manifest themselves as skin problems. These are mostly treatable; the worst side effect is usually that the coat looks unhealthy.

Many problems that are common in many dog breeds are also seen in the Dalmatian. These include elbow dysplasia, hip dysplasia, bloat/gastric torsion, progressive retinal atrophy (PRA), von Willebrand's disease, IgA deficiency and seizures.

Dalmatians that are cared for properly are likely to live long and healthy lives with none of these problems. The best way to keep your Dal healthy is to find a good veterinarian, preferably one who has experience with Dalmatians, and work with him to practice preventative medicine.

Dalmatians do have certain breed-specific problems, but good breeders do their best to keep these problems out of their lines. These well-cared-for pups are kept warm with a heat lamp in their whelping/puppy pen.

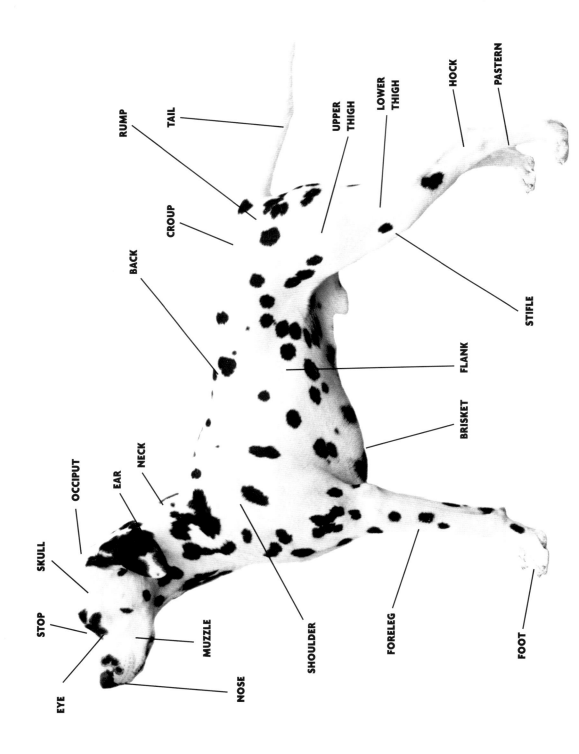

BREED STANDARD FOR THE
DALMATIAN

The American Kennel Club, the main governing body of the canine world in the United States, sets forth a breed standard for each dog breed that it recognizes. The standard is used as a tool: by breeders, in evaluating their dogs and trying to breed the best possible specimen; by judges, in deciding which dogs possess the best conformation in the show ring; and by average breed fanciers, to see how their dogs "measure up." The points of the standard are very specific in describing the perfect dog, so much so that it is impossible to breed a dog that will match every specification exactly. Nonetheless, breed standards are very valuable in ensuring consistency in the breed from generation to generation. Breed standards also serve to safeguard the breed's best qualities—to ensure that each breed does not lose the characteristics, of both form and function, that initially set it apart from other breeds and determined its original purpose.

A breed standard is used as a tool by which the entire dog, both temperament and physical characteristics, is measured and evaluated.

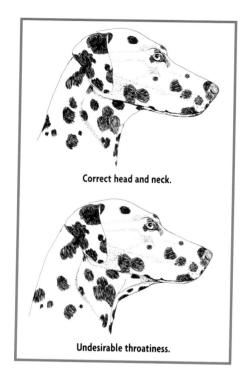

Correct head and neck.

Undesirable throatiness.

FROM THE AMERICAN KENNEL CLUB BREED STANDARD FOR THE DALMATIAN:

General Appearance: The Dalmatian is a distinctively spotted dog; poised and alert; strong, muscular and active; free of shyness; intelligent in expression; symmetrical in outline; and without exaggeration or coarseness. The Dalmatian is capable of great endurance, combined with fair amount of speed.

Size, Proportion, Substance: Desirable height at the withers is between 19 and 23 inches.

Undersize or oversize is a fault. Any dog or bitch over 24 inches at the withers is disqualified. The overall length of the body from the forechest to the buttocks is approximately equal to the height at the withers. The Dalmatian has good substance and is strong and sturdy in bone, but never coarse.

Head: The head is in balance with the overall dog. It is of fair length and is free of loose skin. The Dalmatian's expression is alert and intelligent, indicating a stable and outgoing temperament. The eyes are set moderately well apart, are medium sized and somewhat rounded in appearance, and are set well into the skull. Eye color is brown or blue, or any combination thereof; the darker the better and usually darker in black-spotted than in liver-spotted dogs. Abnormal position of the eyelids or eyelashes (ectropion, entropion, trichiasis) is a major fault. The ears are of moderate size, proportionately wide at the base and gradually tapering to a rounded tip. They are set rather high, and are carried close to the head, and are thin and fine in texture. The top of the skull is flat with a slight vertical furrow and is approximately as wide as it is long. The stop is moderately well defined. The cheeks blend smoothly into a powerful muzzle, the top of which is level and parallel to the top of the skull. The muzzle and the top of the

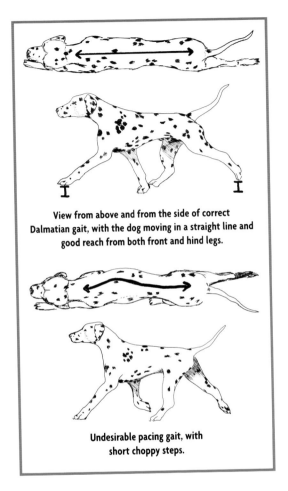

View from above and from the side of correct Dalmatian gait, with the dog moving in a straight line and good reach from both front and hind legs.

Undesirable pacing gait, with short choppy steps.

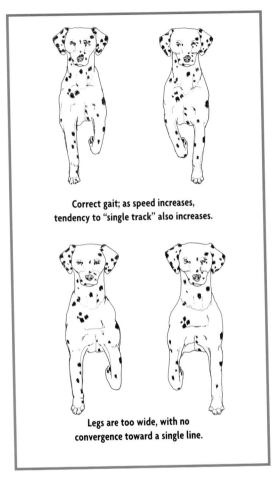

Correct gait; as speed increases, tendency to "single track" also increases.

Legs are too wide, with no convergence toward a single line.

skull are about equal in length. The nose is completely pigmented on the leather, black in black-spotted dogs and brown in liver-spotted dogs. Incomplete nose pigmentation is a major fault. The lips are clean and close fitting. The teeth meet in a scissors bite. Overshot or undershot bites are disqualifications.

Neck, Topline, Body: The neck is nicely arched, fairly long, free from throatiness, and blends smoothly into the shoulders. The topline is smooth. The chest is deep, capacious and of moderate width, having good spring of rib without being barrel shaped. The brisket reaches to the elbow. The underline of the rib cage curves

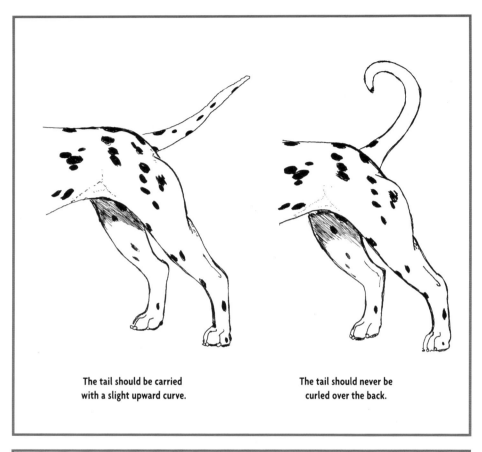

The tail should be carried with a slight upward curve.

The tail should never be curled over the back.

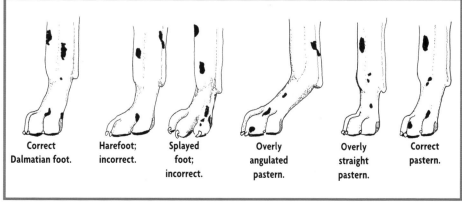

Correct Dalmatian foot.

Harefoot; incorrect.

Splayed foot; incorrect.

Overly angulated pastern.

Overly straight pastern.

Correct pastern.

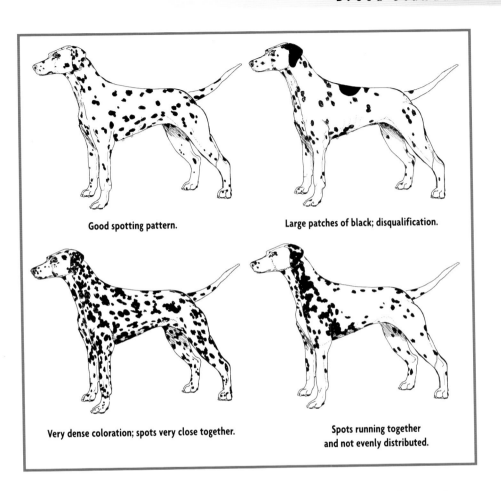

Good spotting pattern.

Large patches of black; disqualification.

Very dense coloration; spots very close together.

Spots running together
and not evenly distributed.

gradually into a moderate tuck-up. The back is level and strong. The loin is short, muscular and slightly arched. The flanks narrow through the loin. The croup is nearly level with the back. The tail is a natural extension of the topline. It is not inserted too low down. Ring tails and low-set tails are faults.

Forequarters: The shoulders are smoothly muscled and well laid back. The elbows are close to the body. The legs are straight, strong and sturdy in bone.

Hindquarters: The hindquarters are powerful, having smooth, yet well defined muscles. The stifle is well bent. The hocks are well let down.

Feet: Feet are very important. Both front and rear feet are round and compact with thick, elastic pads and well arched toes.

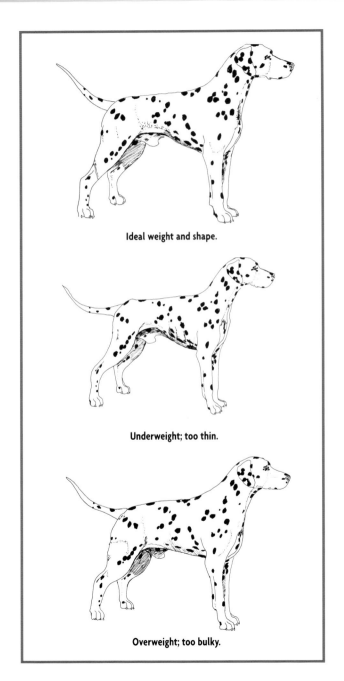

Ideal weight and shape.

Underweight; too thin.

Overweight; too bulky.

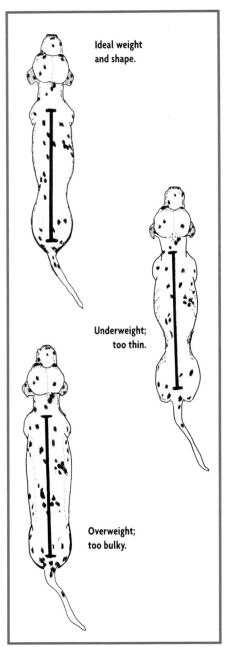

Ideal weight and shape.

Underweight; too thin.

Overweight; too bulky.

Coat: The coat is short, dense, fine and close fitting. It is neither woolly nor silky. It is sleek, glossy and healthy in appearance.

Color and Markings: Color and markings and their overall appearance are very important points to be evaluated. The ground color is pure white. In black-spotted dogs the spots are dense black. In liver-spotted dogs the spots are liver brown. Any color markings other than black or liver are disqualified. Spots are round and well-defined, the more distinct the better. They vary from the size of a dime to the size of a half-dollar. They are pleasingly and evenly distributed. The less the spots intermingle the better. Spots are usually smaller on the head, legs and tail than on the body. Ears are preferably spotted. Tri-color (which occurs rarely in this breed) is a disqualification. It consists of tan markings found on the head, neck, chest, leg or tail of a black- or liver-spotted dog. Bronzing of black spots, and fading and/or darkening of liver spots due to environmental conditions or normal processes of coat change are not tri-coloration. Patches are a disqualification. A patch is a solid mass of black or liver hair containing no white hair. It is appreciably larger than a normal sized spot. Patches are a dense, brilliant color with sharply defined, smooth edges. Patches are present at birth. Large color masses formed by intermingled or overlapping spots are not patches. Such masses should indicate individual spots by uneven edges and/or white hairs scattered throughout the mass.

Gait: In keeping with the Dalmatian's historical use as a coach dog, gait and endurance are of great importance. Movement is steady and effortless. There is a powerful drive from the rear coordinated with extended reach in the front. The topline remains level. Elbows, hocks and feet turn neither in nor out. As the speed of the trot increases, there is a tendency to single track.

Temperament: Temperament is stable and outgoing, yet dignified. Shyness is a major fault.

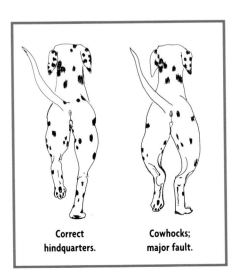

Correct hindquarters.

Cowhocks; major fault.

DALMATIAN

So you're intrigued by the Dalmatian and you have your heart set on adding a new spotted friend to your family. Now what? Where should you begin your search for a perfect pup? The best place to start is by visiting a reputable breeder. It won't be hard to find a litter of Dalmatians, but a word of caution is warranted about selecting a breeder. The Dalmatian is a breed that has fallen prey to commercial breeding for obvious, however unfortunate, reasons. Take a look around and you're sure to "spot" a

PUPPY SELECTION

Your selection of a good puppy can be determined by your needs. A show potential or a good pet? It is your choice. Every puppy, however, should be of good temperament. Although show-quality puppies are bred and raised with emphasis on physical conformation, responsible breeders strive for equally good temperament. Do not buy from a breeder who concentrates solely on physical beauty at the expense of personality.

Bred by a conscientious breeder and reared with love, this Dalmatian baby is ready for a good home.

The majority of Dalmatian breeders is honest, sincere and very knowledgeable. A Dalmatian breed club can refer you to a reputable breeder affiliated with the club.

Dal: in the movies, on television, in print advertising, etc. The Dal's distinctive appearance and exuberant personality make him a natural star! But fame is not without its pitfalls—all of a sudden everybody wants a Dalmatian, and thus begins a vicious cycle of supply and demand. This boom in business is a good thing when dealing with merchandise, but puppies are not merchandise. They are living creatures that cannot be churned out factory-style, despite some less-than-conscientious breeders' assembly-line approach to breeding.

As a result, too many breeders have focused on producing as many puppies as possible, with no regard for the quality and health of the parents or that of the resulting pups. This is not at all meant to discredit the many reputable Dalmatian breeders that have the best interest of the breed in mind. In fact, this recent surge in overbreeding has only led those involved in the breed to become more stringent in their breeding programs and to educate the

RELEASE ME
Breeders rarely release puppies until they are eight to ten weeks of age. This is an acceptable age for most breeds of dog, excepting toy breeds, which are not released until around 12 weeks, given their petite sizes. If a breeder has a puppy that is 12 weeks or more, it is likely well socialized and housebroken. Be sure that it is otherwise healthy before deciding to take it home.

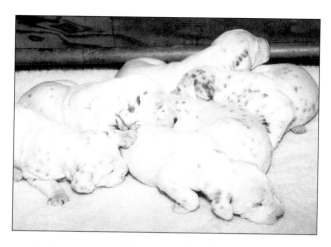

A pile of snoozing pups makes an adorable picture! These pups will stay with the breeder until about eight weeks of age, when they will be fully weaned and ready for new homes.

the major reason that you should find a breeder who only breeds from healthy dogs that have been tested as free of physical defects, and who will be a source of help and advice as you raise your Dalmatian.

Well, now that we have the serious part out of the way, it's time to start the fun. First of all, where do you find a good breeder? Breed clubs, like the DCA, kennel clubs and dog shows are good places to start. Clubs often have breeder referrals and puppy lists, and they can put you in touch with someone in your area. Alternatively, you can seek them out yourself. Go to a dog show, watch the Dalmatians and approach the owners of the dogs you like. If the owner is not the breeder, the owner can put you in touch with the breeder. People who love Dalmatians will usually be more than happy to talk to you about their spotted friends.

public about the dangers of irresponsible breeding.

It is this type of breeder, the type of person who is truly committed to protecting the health and quality of the Dalmatian, whom you need to seek out in your quest for a puppy. The Dalmatian is a breed that is prone to some peculiar health problems. These are problems that a pet owner can manage easily with a bit of preventative care, but this is

Upon meeting the breeder, don't think it strange if you are subject to an onslaught of questions. You want to make sure that everything checks out with the breeder, and vice versa. One trait of a good breeder is that he or she wants to make sure that you will provide a proper home for the puppy. Don't be insulted—be reassured that the breeder cares!

The next step is for you to meet a litter of puppies, and what a test of willpower that will be! It's

PUPPY APPEARANCE
Your puppy should have a well-fed appearance but not a distended abdomen, which may indicate worms or incorrect feeding, or both. The body should be firm, with a solid feel. The skin of the abdomen should be pale pink and clean, without signs of scratching or rash. Check the hind legs to make certain that dewclaws were removed, if any were present at birth.

nearly impossible to look at a litter of spotted babies and not want to scoop them up and bring all of them home…they're absolutely irresistible. So don't completely deny yourself. Let yourself get caught up in the overwhelming puppy cuteness for a few minutes, but then snap out of it! While the puppy you choose will be a pet that you will love for years to come, now is not the time to let your heart rule your head. You are making an important decision, so please take it seriously.

Observing a litter lets you see the pups in action. You'll get a chance to see each one's personality and its role in the litter. It will also let you see how the pups are cared for, if their quarters are kept clean, if they look healthy, etc. Try to see at least one of the pups' parents too, as this will give you an idea of the pups' eventual looks and temperaments.

Perhaps the most important thing you can ask a Dalmatian breeder is, "Have the parents and pups been BAER tested?" Brainstem Auditory Evoked Response (BAER) testing is the only sure way to know if the dogs have normal hearing, as deafness is a major concern in the breed. Ask for proof of the test results, and don't accept the breeder's word alone that the dogs are fine. Even if both parents have normal hearing, they may carry genes for deafness, which can be passed to

Your child, if you have one, must bond with the puppy and learn how to treat him with care.

the offspring. While a unilaterally deaf (in one ear) Dalmatian may make a fine pet, a bilaterally deaf (in both ears) Dal is

BOY OR GIRL?

An important consideration to be discussed is the sex of your puppy. For a family companion, a bitch may be the better choice, considering the female's inbred concern for all young creatures and her accompanying tolerance and patience. It is always advised to spay a pet bitch, which may guarantee her a longer life.

> **FINANCIAL RESPONSIBILITY**
> Grooming tools, collars, leashes, dog beds and, of course, toys will be an expense to you when you first obtain your pup, and the cost will trickle on throughout your dog's lifetime. If your puppy damages or destroys your possessions or something belonging to a neighbor, you can calculate additional expense. There is also veterinary expenses plus flea and pest control, which every dog owner faces more than once. You must be able to handle the financial responsibility of owning a dog.

Although the Dalmatian needs to spend time outdoors and to exercise, he loves being in the house and around his owners.

likely too much to handle for the average pet-owning family.

If you're not comfortable with the breeder and you haven't yet found the pup for you, keep looking. Remember, your Dalmatian will be part of your family for at least ten, maybe even fifteen, years, and you will want to stay in touch with the breeder. You may need advice about raising your Dalmatian, and the breeder will likely want to check up on the pup's progress and how the pup is getting along in your family. For this, you want to choose a helpful breeder to whom you feel comfortable talking.

Be prepared to wait for a good-quality pup. Many breeders have waiting lists or a litter may not be available immediately. Be patient, and soon you will find the

Dalmatian that perfectly suits you and your family.

COMMITMENT OF OWNERSHIP
After considering all of these factors, you obviously already have made some very important decisions about selecting your puppy. You have chosen a Dalmatian, which means that you have decided which characteristics you want in a dog and what type of dog will best fit into your family and lifestyle. If you have selected a breeder, you have gone a step further—you have done your research and found a responsible, conscientious person who breeds quality Dalmatians and who should be a reliable source of help as you and your puppy adjust to life together. If you have observed a litter in action, you have obtained a firsthand look at the

dynamics of a puppy "pack" and, thus, you should learn about each pup's individual personality— perhaps you have even found one that particularly appeals to you (when you've found the pup for you, you'll know it!).

Researching your breed, selecting a responsible breeder and observing as many pups as possible are all important steps on the way to dog ownership. It may seem like a lot of effort...and you have not even brought the pup home yet! Remember, though, you cannot be too careful when it comes to deciding on the type of dog you want and finding out about your prospective pup's background. Buying a puppy is not—or should not be—just another whimsical purchase. This is one instance in which you actually *do* get to choose your own family! You may be thinking that buying a puppy should be fun—it should not be so serious and so much work. Keep in mind that your puppy is not a cuddly stuffed toy or decorative lawn ornament, but a creature that will become a real member of your family. You will come to realize that, while buying a puppy is a pleasurable and exciting endeavor, it is not something to be taken lightly. Relax...the fun will start when the pup comes home!

Always keep in mind that a puppy is nothing more than a baby in a furry disguise...a baby who is virtually helpless in a human world and who trusts his owner for fulfillment of his basic needs for survival. In addition to water and shelter, your pup needs care, protection, guidance and love. If you are not prepared to commit to this, then you are not prepared to own a dog.

Wait a minute, you say. How hard could this be? All of my

PEDIGREE VS. REGISTRATION CERTIFICATE

Too often new owners are confused between these two important documents. Your puppy's pedigree, essentially a family tree, is a written record of a dog's genealogy of three generations or more. The pedigree will show you the names as well as performance titles of all the dogs in your pup's background. Your breeder must provide you with a registration application, with his part properly filled out. You must complete the application and send it to the AKC with the proper fee. For AKC registration, the puppy must come from a litter that has been AKC-registered by the breeder, born in the USA and from a sire and dam that are also registered with the AKC.

The seller must provide you with complete records to identify the puppy including: breed; sex; date of birth; litter number (when available); names and registration numbers of the parents; breeder's name; and date sold or delivered.

Decide on the rules from the beginning. If you don't want your Dalmatian on the furniture, teach him so before he becomes accustomed to a favorite spot.

your Dalmatian puppy home. You will also have to prepare your home and family for the new addition. Much as you would prepare a nursery for a newborn baby, you will need to designate a place in your home that will be the puppy's own. How you prepare your home will depend on how much freedom the dog will be allowed. Will he be confined to one room or a specific area in the house, or will he be allowed to roam as he pleases? Whatever you decide, you must ensure that he has a place that he can "call his own."

When you bring your new puppy into your home, you are bringing him into what will become his home as well. Obviously, you did not buy a puppy so that he could "rule the roost" in your house, but in order for a puppy to grow into a stable, well-adjusted dog, he has to feel

neighbors own dogs and they seem to be doing just fine. Why should I have to worry about all of this? Well, you should not worry about it; in fact, you will probably find that once your Dalmatian pup gets used to his new home, he will fall into his place in the family quite naturally. But it never hurts to emphasize the commitment of dog ownership. With some time and patience, it is really not too difficult to raise a curious and exuberant Dalmatian pup to be a well-adjusted and well-mannered adult dog—a dog that could be your most loyal friend.

PREPARING PUPPY'S PLACE IN YOUR HOME
Researching your breed and finding a breeder are only two aspects of the "homework" you will have to do before bringing

PUPPY PROBLEMS
The majority of problems that are commonly seen in young pups will disappear as your dog gets older. However, how you deal with problems when he is young will determine how he reacts to discipline as an adult dog. It is important to establish who is boss (hopefully it will be you!) right away when you are first bonding with your dog. This bond will set the tone for the rest of your life together.

comfortable in his surroundings. Remember, he is leaving the warmth and security of his mother and littermates, as well as the familiarity of the only place he has ever known, so it is important to make his transition as easy as possible. By preparing a place in your home for the puppy, you are making him feel as welcome as possible in a strange new place. It should not take him long to get used to it, but the sudden shock of being transplanted is somewhat traumatic for a young pup. Imagine how a small child would feel in the same situation—that is how your puppy must be feeling. It is up to you to reassure him and to let him know, "Little fellow, you are going to like it here!"

ARE YOU PREPARED?

Unfortunately, when a puppy is bought by someone who does not take into consideration the time and attention that dog ownership requires, it is the puppy who suffers when he is either abandoned or placed in a shelter by a frustrated owner. So all of the "homework" you do in preparation for your pup's arrival will benefit you both. The more informed you are, the more you will know what to expect and the better equipped you will be to handle the ups and downs of raising a puppy. Hopefully, everyone in the household is willing to do his part in raising and caring for the pup. The anticipation of owning a dog often brings a lot of promises from excited family members: "I will walk him every day," "I will feed him," "I will housebreak him," etc., but these things take time and effort, and promises can easily be forgotten once the novelty of the new pet has worn off.

You've made the decision…you've selected your Dalmatian puppy. Now what? Have you purchased a crate and all the other necessities of life for a dog?

WHAT YOU SHOULD BUY

CRATE

To someone unfamiliar with the use of crates in dog training, it may seem like punishment to shut a dog in a crate, but this is not the case at all. Crates are not cruel—crates have many humane and highly effective uses in dog care and training. For example, crate training is a very popular and very successful housebreaking method.

Crates can be purchased at your local pet shop. The pet shop will offer a variety of sizes, styles and colors. Purchase a sturdy crate that is large enough for a fully-grown Dalmatian.

PHOTO COURTESY OF MIKKI PET PRODUCTS.

Wire crates are good for use in the home, as they afford the dog a view of what's going on around him. If your dog likes a more private atmosphere, simply drape a towel or small carpet over the crate. A pet shop can usually order any size crate that you need.

A crate can also keep your dog safe during travel and, perhaps most importantly, a crate provides your dog with a place of his own in your home. It serves as a "doggie bedroom" of sorts—your Dalmatian can curl up in his crate when he wants to sleep or when he just needs a break. Many dogs sleep in their crates overnight. When lined with soft blankets and a favorite toy, a crate becomes a cozy pseudo-den for your dog. Like his ancestors, he too will seek out the comfort and retreat of a den—you just happen to be providing him with a safe, clean place to call his own.

As far as purchasing a crate, the type that you buy is up to you. It will most likely be one of the two most popular types: wire or fiberglass. There are advantages and disadvantages to each type. For example, a wire crate is more open, allowing the air to flow through and affording the dog a view of what is going on around him, while a fiberglass crate is sturdier. Both can double as travel crates, providing protection for the dog. The size of the crate is

another thing to consider. Puppies do not stay puppies forever, and sometimes it seems as if they grow right before your eyes! Your Dalmatian will outgrow a puppy-sized crate rather quickly, so purchase a large crate that will last him into adulthood.

BEDDING

Padding or cushions in the dog's crate will help the dog feel more at home, and you may also put in a small blanket. This will take the place of the leaves, twigs, etc., that the pup would instinctively use in the wild to make a den; the pup can make his own "burrow" in the crate. Although your pup is far removed from his den-making ancestors, the denning instinct is still a part of his genetic makeup. Secondly, until you bring your pup home, he has been sleeping amid the warmth of his mother and littermates, and while a blanket is not the same as a warm,

breathing body, it still provides heat and something with which to snuggle. You will want to wash your pup's bedding frequently in case he has an accident in his crate, and replace or remove any bedding that becomes ragged and starts to fall apart.

A bed with soft padding is an excellent choice for the new puppy. Offer the puppy a safe chew toy to take his mind off spending his first nights away from his mother and siblings.

TOYS

Toys are a must for dogs of all ages, especially for curious playful pups. Puppies are the "children" of the dog world, and what child does not love toys? Chew toys provide enjoyment to both dog and owner—your dog will enjoy playing with his favorite toys, while you will enjoy the fact that they distract him from your expensive shoes and leather couch. Puppies love to chew; in fact, chewing is a physical need for pups as they are teething, and everything looks appetizing! The full range of your possessions—from old dishcloth to Oriental rug—are fair game in the eyes of a

SPECIAL TRAINING

Training your puppy takes much patience and can be frustrating at times, but you should see results from your efforts. If you have a puppy that seems untrainable, take him to a trainer or behaviorist. The dog may have a personality problem that requires the help of a professional, or perhaps you need help in learning how to train your dog.

teething pup. Puppies are not all that discerning when it comes to finding something to literally "sink their teeth into"—everything tastes great!

Only the strongest, most durable toys should be offered to your Dalmatian. Breeders advise owners to resist stuffed toys, because they can become de-stuffed in no time. The overly excited pup may ingest the stuffing, which is neither nutritious nor digestible.

Similarly, squeaky toys are quite popular, but must be avoided for the Dalmatian. Perhaps a squeaky toy can be used as an aid in training, but not for free play. If a pup "disembowels" one of these, the small plastic squeaker inside can be dangerous if swallowed. Monitor the condition of all your pup's toys carefully and get rid of any that have been chewed to the point of becoming potentially dangerous.

Be careful of natural bones, which have a tendency to splinter into sharp, dangerous pieces. Also

Pet shops offer a variety of toys made especially for dogs. The toys shown here are some examples. *Do not use human toys for dogs.* They are too fragile and may contain dyes that are toxic to canines.

be careful of rawhide, which can turn into pieces that are easy to swallow or into a mushy mess on your carpet.

LEAD

A nylon lead is probably the best option, as it is the most resistant to puppy teeth should your pup take a liking to chewing on his lead. Of course, this is a habit that should be nipped in the bud, but if your pup likes to chew on his lead, he has a very slim chance of being able to chew through the strong nylon. Nylon leads are also lightweight, which is good for a young Dalmatian who is just getting used to the idea of walking on a lead. For everyday walking and safety purposes, the nylon lead is a good choice. As your pup grows up and gets used to walking

on the lead, you may want to purchase a flexible lead. These leads allow you to extend the length to give the dog a broader area to explore or to shorten the length to keep the dog close to you. Of course there are special leads for training purposes, but these are not necessary for routine walks.

COLLAR

Your pup should get used to wearing a collar all the time since you will want to attach his ID tags to it; plus, you have to attach the lead to something! A lightweight nylon collar is a good choice; make sure that it fits snugly enough so that the pup cannot

Most trainers recommend using a strong yet lightweight nylon lead for routine walks. Pet shops usually have a wide selection of leads.

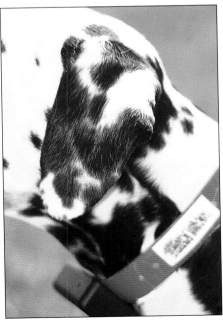

A collar with an electronic device attached can enable the dog to be restrained within a given area. This is also known as electrical fencing.

CHOOSE AN APPROPRIATE COLLAR

The **BUCKLE COLLAR** is the standard collar used for everyday purposes. Be sure that you adjust the buckle on growing puppies. Check it every day. It can become too tight overnight! These collars can be made of leather or nylon. Attach your dog's identification tags to this collar.

The **CHOKE COLLAR** is designed for use *only* during training. It is constructed of highly polished steel so that it slides easily through the stainless steel loop. The idea is that the dog controls the pressure around his neck and he will stop pulling if the collar becomes uncomfortable.

The **HALTER** is for a trained dog that has to be restrained to prevent running away, chasing a cat and the like. Considered the most humane of all collars, it is frequently used on smaller dogs on which collars are not comfortable.

A thin lead like this is the type used in the show ring, but is not strong enough for everyday use.

Browse your pet shop's selection of bowls for your dog's food and water, and purchase sturdy bowls for your Dalmatian. Elevated bowl stands are also recommended as a bloat preventative.

wriggle out of it, but is loose enough so that it will not be uncomfortably tight around the pup's neck. You should be able to fit a finger between the pup and the collar. It may take some time for your pup to get used to wearing the collar, but soon he will not even notice that it is there. Choke collars are made for training, but should only be used by an experienced handler.

FOOD AND WATER BOWLS

Your pup will need two bowls, one for food and one for water. You may want two sets of bowls, one for inside and one for outside,

PHOTO COURTESY OF MIKKI PET PRODUCTS.

Heavy plastic or stainless steel bowls are recommended for Dalmatians.

constantly chewing apart his bowl (for his safety and for your wallet!). Also purchase stands on which to elevate the bowls; this is proven to reduce the risk of bloat.

CLEANING SUPPLIES
Until a pup is housebroken, you will be doing a lot of cleaning. "Accidents" will occur, which is okay in the beginning because the

depending on where the dog will be fed and where he will be spending most of his time. Stainless steel or sturdy plastic bowls are popular choices. Plastic bowls are more chewable, but dogs tend not to chew on the steel variety, which can be sterilized. It is important to buy sturdy bowls since anything is in danger of being chewed by puppy teeth and you do not want your dog to be

> ## QUALITY FOOD
> The cost of food must also be mentioned. All dogs need a good-quality food with an adequate supply of protein to develop their bones and muscles properly. Most dogs are not picky eaters but, unless fed properly, can quickly succumb to skin problems.

Even a sturdy bowl can take a beating from a hungry Dalmatian puppy.

puppy does not know any better. All you can do is be prepared to clean up any accidents. Old rags, towels, newspapers and a safe disinfectant are good to have on hand.

BEYOND THE BASICS
The items previously discussed are the bare necessities. You will find out what else you need as you go along—grooming supplies, flea/tick protection, baby gates to partition a room, etc. These things will vary depending on your situation, but it is important that you have everything you need to

feed your Dalmatian and make him comfortable in his first few days at home.

PUPPY-PROOFING YOUR HOME

Aside from making sure that your Dalmatian will be comfortable in your home, you also have to make sure that your home is safe for your Dalmatian. This means taking precautions so that your pup will not get into anything he should not get into and that there is nothing within his reach that may harm him should he sniff it, chew it, inspect it, etc. This probably seems obvious since, while you are primarily concerned with your pup's safety, at the same time you do not want your belong-

ings to be ruined. Breakables should be placed out of reach if your dog is to have full run of the house. It's amazing how quickly a wagging Dal tail can unintentionally sweep a table clean! If he is to be limited to certain places within the house, keep any potentially dangerous items in the "off-limits" areas. An electrical cord can pose a danger should the puppy decide to taste it—and who is going to convince a pup that it would not make a great chew toy? Cords should be fastened tightly against the wall. If your dog is going to spend time in a crate, make sure that there is nothing near his crate that he can reach if he sticks his curious little nose or paws through the openings. Just as you would with a child, keep all household cleaners and chemicals where the pup cannot get to them.

It is also important to make sure that the outside of your home is safe. Of course your puppy should never be unsupervised, but a pup let loose in the yard will

The responsible dog owner cleans up the droppings of his Dalmatian. Your local pet shop will have proper "poop-scoop" devices to assist you in this task.

PUPPY-PROOFING

Thoroughly puppy-proof your house before bringing your puppy home. Never use roach or rodent poisons in any area accessible to the puppy. Avoid the use of toilet bowl cleaners. Most dogs are born with toilet bowl "sonar" and will take a drink if the lid is left open. Also keep the trash secured and out of reach.

CHEMICAL TOXINS

Scour your garage for potential puppy dangers. Remove weed killers, pesticides and antifreeze materials. Antifreeze is highly toxic and just a few drops can kill even a large dog. The sweet taste attracts the animal, who will quickly consume it from the floor or curbside.

want to run and explore, and he should be granted that freedom. Do not let a fence give you a false sense of security; you would be surprised how crafty (and persistent) a dog can be in figuring out how to dig under and squeeze his way through small holes, or to jump or climb over a fence. The remedy is to make the fence high enough so that it really is impossible for your dog to get over it (about 5 feet should suffice), and well embedded into the ground. Be sure to repair or secure any gaps in the fence. Check the fence periodically to ensure that it is in good shape and make repairs as needed; a very determined pup may return to the same spot to "work on it" until he is able to get through.

FIRST TRIP TO THE VET

You have picked out your puppy, and your home and family are ready. Now all you have to do is collect your Dalmatian from the breeder and the fun begins, right?

Well...not so fast. Something else you need to prepare is your pup's first trip to the veterinarian. Perhaps the breeder can recommend someone in the area who specializes in Dalmatians, or maybe you know some other Dalmatian owners who can suggest a good vet. Either way, it is important to choose a vet who is familiar with the idiosyncrasies of Dalmatian health. You should have an appointment arranged for your pup before you pick him up and plan on taking him for an examination before bringing him home.

The pup's first visit will consist of an overall examination to make sure that the pup does not have any problems that are not apparent to you. The veterinarian will also set up a schedule for the pup's vaccinations; the breeder will inform you of which ones the pup has already received and the vet can continue from there.

INTRODUCTION TO THE FAMILY

Everyone in the house will be excited about the puppy's coming home and will want to pet him and play with him, but it is best to make the introduction low-key so as not to overwhelm the puppy. He is apprehensive already. It is the first time he has been separated from his mother and the breeder, and the ride to your home is likely the first time he has been in a car. The last thing you want to do is smother

family members or may busy himself with exploring for a while. Gradually, each person should spend some time with the pup, one at a time, crouching down to get as close to the pup's level as possible and letting him sniff their hands and petting him gently. He definitely needs human attention and he needs to be touched—this is how to form an immediate bond. Just remember that the pup is experiencing a lot of things for the first time, at the same time. There are new people, new noises, new smells and new things to investigate: so be gentle, be affectionate and be as comforting as you can be.

Dalmatians are curious and they like to chew, which could be a dangerous combination. If you allow your Dalmatian freedom in the yard, be sure your yard is safe from any object that could cause your dog harm.

him, as this will only frighten him further. This is not to say that human contact is not extremely necessary at this stage, because this is the time when a connection between the pup and his human family is formed. Gentle petting and soothing words should help console him, as well as just putting him down and letting him explore on his own (under your watchful eye, of course).

The pup may approach the

NATURAL TOXINS

Examine your grass and landscaping before bringing your puppy home. Many varieties of plants have leaves, stems or flowers that are toxic if ingested, and you can depend on a curious puppy to investigate them. Ask your vet for information on poisonous plants or research them at your library.

If you see your dog carrying a piece of vegetation in his mouth, approach him in a quiet, disinterested manner, avoid eye contact, pet him and gradually remove the plant from his mouth. Alternatively, offer him a treat and maybe he'll drop the plant on his own accord. Be sure no toxic plants are growing in your own yard or kept in your home.

Your puppy's first day in his new home will be spent investigating all the sites that might be used for relieving himself. You can start training him right away to use a specific spot in the yard.

YOUR PUP'S FIRST NIGHT HOME

You have traveled home with your new charge safely in his basket or crate. He's been to the vet for a thorough check-up: he's been weighed, his papers have been examined, perhaps he's even been vaccinated and wormed as well. He's met the whole family…and he's licked the whole family, including the excited children and the less-than-happy cat. He's explored his area, his new bed, the yard and anywhere else he's been permitted. He's eaten his first meal at home and relieved himself in the proper place. He's heard lots of new sounds, smelled new friends and seen more of the outside world than ever before.

That was just the first day! He's worn out and is ready for bed…or so you think!

It's puppy's first night and you are ready to say "Good night." Keep in mind that this is puppy's first night ever to be sleeping alone. His dam and littermates are no longer at paw's length and he's a bit scared, cold and lonely. Be reassuring to your new family member. This is not the time to spoil him and give in to his inevitable whining.

Puppies whine. They whine to let the others know where they are and hopefully to get company out of it. Place your pup in his new bed or crate in his room and close the door. Mercifully, he may fall asleep without a peep. If the inevitable occurs, ignore the whining; he is fine. Be strong and keep his best interest in mind. Do not allow your heart to become guilty and visit the pup. He will fall asleep.

Many breeders recommend placing a piece of bedding from his former home in his new bed so that he recognizes the scent of his litter-mates. Others still advise placing a

THE RIDE HOME

Taking your dog from the breeder to your home in a car can be a very uncomfortable experience for both of you. The puppy will have been taken from his warm, friendly, safe environment and brought into a strange new environment. An environment that moves! Be prepared for loose bowels, urination, crying, whining and even fear biting. With proper love and encouragement when you arrive home, the stress of the trip should disappear quickly.

A well-socialized Dalmatian will accept new pets into the household as long as careful introductions are made.

hot water bottle in his bed for warmth. The latter may be a good idea provided the pup doesn't attempt to suckle—he'll get good and wet and may not fall asleep so fast.

Puppy's first night can be somewhat stressful for the pup and his new family. Remember that you are setting the tone of nighttime at your house. Unless you want to play with your pup every night at 10 p.m., midnight and 2 a.m., don't initiate the habit. Your family will thank you, and so will your pup!

PREVENTING PUPPY PROBLEMS

SOCIALIZATION

Now that you have done all of the preparatory work and have helped your pup get accustomed to his new home and family, it is about time for you to have some fun! Socializing your Dalmatian pup gives you the opportunity to show off your new

STRESS-FREE

Some experts in canine health advise that stress during a dog's early years of development can compromise and weaken his immune system and may trigger the potential for a shortened life expectancy. They emphasize the need for happy and stress-free growing-up years.

When a dog is introduced to another dog, there is often a struggle for dominance. Who is going to be the leader of the pack? For this reason, it is best to keep dogs that are meeting for the first time on lead.

friend, and your pup gets to reap the benefits of being an adorable furry spotted creature that people will want to pet and, in general, think is absolutely precious!

Besides getting to know his new family, your puppy should be exposed to other people, animals and situations, but of course he must not come into close contact with dogs you don't know well until his course of injections is fully completed.

Socialization will help him become well adjusted as he grows up and less prone to being timid or fearful of the new things he will encounter. Your pup's socialization

began at the breeder's, but now it is your responsibility to continue it. The socialization he receives up until the age of 12 weeks is the

SOCIALIZATION

Thorough socialization includes not only meeting new people but also being introduced to new experiences such as riding in the car, having his coat brushed, hearing the television, walking in a crowd—the list is endless. The more your pup experiences, and the more positive the experiences are, the less of a shock and the less scary it will be for your pup to encounter new things.

most critical, as this is the time when he forms his impressions of the outside world. Be especially careful during the eight-to-ten-week old period, also known as the fear period. The interaction he receives during this time should be gentle and reassuring. Lack of socialization can manifest itself in fear and aggression as the dog grows up. He needs lots of human contact, affection, handling and exposure to other animals.

Once your pup has received his necessary vaccinations, feel free to take him out and about (on his lead, of course). Walk him around the neighborhood, take him on your daily errands, let people pet him, let him meet other dogs and pets, etc. Puppies do not have to try to make friends; there will be no shortage of people who will want to introduce themselves. Just make sure that you carefully supervise each meeting. If the neighborhood children want to say hello, for example, that is great—children and pups most often make great companions. However, sometimes an excited child can unintentionally handle a pup too roughly, or an overzealous pup can playfully nip a little too hard. You want to make socialization experiences positive ones. What a pup learns during this very formative stage will impact his attitude toward future encounters. You want your dog to be comfortable around everyone. A pup that has a bad experience with a child

MANNERS MATTER

During the socialization process, a puppy should meet people, experience different environments and definitely be exposed to other canines. Through playing and interacting with other dogs, your puppy will learn lessons, ranging from controlling the pressure of his jaws by biting his littermates to the inner-workings of the canine pack, that he will apply to his human relationships for the rest of his life. That is why removing a puppy from its litter too early (before eight weeks) can be detrimental to the pup's development.

may grow up to be a dog that is shy around or aggressive toward children.

CONSISTENCY IN TRAINING

Dogs, being pack animals, naturally need a leader, or else they try to

A puppy's behavior is shaped from day one. Young pups learn many essential lessons from their mother, litter-mates and breeder before they leave for new homes.

establish dominance in their packs. When you bring a dog into your family, the choice of who becomes the leader and who becomes the "pack" is entirely up to you! Your pup's intuitive quest for dominance, coupled with the fact that it is nearly impossible to look at an adorable young Dalmatian with his "puppy-dog" eyes and not cave in, give the pup almost an unfair advantage in getting the upper hand! A pup will definitely test the waters to see what he can and cannot do. Do not give in to those pleading eyes—stand your ground when it comes to disciplining the pup and make sure that all family members do the same. It will only confuse the pup when Mother tells him to get off the couch when he is used to sitting up there with Father to watch the nightly news. Avoid discrepancies by having all members of the household decide on the rules before the pup even comes home...

and be consistent in enforcing them! Early training shapes the dog's personality, so you cannot be unclear in what you expect.

COMMON PUPPY PROBLEMS
The best way to prevent puppy problems is to be proactive in stopping an undesirable behavior as soon as it starts. The old saying "You can't teach an old dog new tricks" does not necessarily hold true, but it is true that it is much easier to discourage bad behavior in a young developing pup than to wait until the pup's bad behavior becomes the adult dog's bad habit. There are some problems that are especially prevalent in puppies as they develop.

TOYS, TOYS, TOYS
With a big variety of dog toys available, and so many that look like they would be a lot of fun for a dog, be careful in your selection. It is amazing what a set of puppy teeth can do to an innocent-looking toy, so, obviously, safety is a major consideration. Be sure to choose the most durable products that you can find. Hard nylon bones and toys are a safe bet, and many of them are offered in different scents and flavors that will be sure to capture your dog's attention. It is always fun to play a game of catch with your dog, and there are balls and flying discs that are specially made to withstand dog teeth.

NIPPING

As puppies start to teethe, they feel the need to sink their teeth into anything available...unfortunately that includes your fingers, arms, hair, and toes. You may find this behavior cute for the first five seconds...until you feel just how sharp those puppy teeth are. This is something you want to discourage immediately and consistently with a firm "No!" (or whatever number of firm "No's" it takes for him to understand that you mean business). Then replace your finger with an appropriate chew toy. While nipping is merely annoying

When you leave your dog alone, he is best left in his crate. Training your dog to the crate when he is very young will usually result in his accepting his crate whenever he is left alone.

when the dog is young, it can become dangerous as your Dalmatian's adult teeth grow in and his jaws develop. He does not mean any harm, but also doesn't know his own strength.

CRYING/WHINING

Your pup will often cry, whine, whimper, howl or make some type of commotion when he is left alone. This is basically his way of calling out for attention to make sure that you know he is there and that you have not forgotten about him. He feels insecure when he is left alone, when you are out of the house and he is in his crate or when you are in another part of the house and he cannot see you. The noise he is making is an expression of the anxiety he feels at being alone, so he needs to be taught that being alone is okay. You are not actually training the

CRATE-TRAINING TIPS

During crate training, you should partition off the section of the crate in which the pup stays. If he is given too big an area, this will hinder your training efforts. Crate training is based on the fact that a dog does not like to soil his sleeping quarters, so it is ineffective to keep a pup in a crate that is so big that he can eliminate in one end and get far enough away from it to sleep. Also, you want to make the crate den-like for the pup. Blankets and a favorite toy will make the crate cozy for the small pup; as he grows, you may want to evict some of his "roommates" to make more room.

It will take some coaxing at first, but be patient. Given some time to get used to it, your pup will adapt to his new home-within-a-home quite nicely.

dog to stop making noise, you are training him to feel comfortable when he is alone and thus removing the need for him to make the noise. This is where the crate filled with cozy bedding and toys comes in handy. You want to know that he is safe when you are not there to supervise, and you know that he will be safe in his crate rather than roaming freely about the house. In order for the pup to stay in his crate without making a fuss, he needs to be comfortable in his crate. On that note, it is extremely important that the crate is never used as a form of punishment, or the pup will have a negative association with the crate.

Accustom the pup to the crate in short, gradually increasing time intervals in which you put him in the crate, maybe with a treat, and stay in the room with him. If he

PUPPY FEEDING TIPS
You will probably start feeding your pup the same food that he has been getting from the breeder; the breeder should give you a few days' supply to start you off. Although you should not give your pup too many treats, you will want to have puppy treats on hand for coaxing, training, rewards, etc. Be careful, though, as a small pup's calorie requirements are relatively low and a few treats can add up to almost a full day's worth of calories without the required nutrition.

cries or makes a fuss, do not go to him, but stay in his sight. Gradually he will realize that staying in his crate is all right without your help, and it will not be so traumatic for him when you are not around. You may want to leave the radio on softly when you leave the house; the sound of human voices may be comforting to him.

Above all else, your new Dalmatian puppy needs your love, affection and attention. If you are unable or unwilling to devote the necessary energy to a dog, do not bring one home.

CHEWING TIPS

Chewing goes hand in hand with nipping in the sense that a teething puppy is always looking for a way to soothe his aching gums. In this case, instead of chewing on you, he may have taken a liking to your favorite shoe or something else which he should not be chewing. Again, realize that this is a normal canine behavior that does not need to be discouraged, only redirected. Your pup just needs to be taught what is acceptable to chew on and what is off limits. Consistently tell him "No" when you catch him chewing on something forbidden and give him a chew toy. Conversely, praise him when you catch him chewing on something appropriate. In this way, you are discouraging the inappropriate behavior and reinforcing the desired behavior. The puppy chewing should stop after his adult teeth have come in, but an adult dog continues to chew for various reasons—perhaps because he is bored, perhaps to relieve tension or perhaps he just likes to chew. That is why it is important to redirect his chewing when he is still young.

DIETARY AND FEEDING CONSIDERATIONS

Today the choices of food for your Dalmatian are many and varied. There are simply dozens of brands of food in all sorts of flavors and textures, ranging from puppy diets to those for seniors. There are even hypoallergenic and low-calorie diets available. Because your Dalmatian's food has a bearing on coat, health and temperament, it is essential that the most suitable diet is selected for a Dalmatian of his age. A major consideration in feeding the Dalmatian is that a diet excessive in protein, especially proteins high in purines (found mainly in meat and meat by-products), adds to the Dalmatian's natural tendency to form urinary stones. All of this makes choosing the best food for your Dal truly overwhelming. It is not surprising that even the most dedicated owners can be perplexed by choosing the proper diet for their Dalmatians. Only understanding what is best for your dog will help you reach an informed decision.

Dog foods are produced in three basic types: dry, semi-moist and canned. Dry foods are useful for the cost-conscious, for overall they tend to be less expensive than semi-moist or canned. Dry foods contain the least fat and the most preservatives. In general, canned foods are made up of 60–70 percent water, while semi-moist foods often contain so much sugar that they are perhaps the

FOOD PREFERENCE

Selecting the best dry dog food is difficult. There is no majority consensus among veterinary scientists as to the value of nutrient analyses (protein, fat, fiber, moisture, ash, cholesterol, minerals, etc.). All agree that feeding trials are what matter, but you also have to consider the individual dog. Its weight, age and activity, and what pleases its taste all must be considered. It is probably best to take the advice of your veterinarian. Every dog's dietary requirements vary, even during the lifetime of a particular dog.

If your dog is fed a good dry food, it does not require supplements of meat or vegetables. In fact, giving table scraps to a Dalmatian is very dangerous to its health. Dogs do appreciate a little variety in their diets, so you may choose to stay with the same brand but vary the flavor.

having selected ones with plenty of milk. This early milk supply is important in providing colostrum to protect the puppies during the first eight to ten weeks of their lives. Although a mother's milk is much better than any milk formula, despite there being some excellent ones available, if the puppies do not feed, the breeder will have to feed them himself. For those with less experience, advice from a veterinarian is important so that not only the right quantity of milk is fed but

Puppies are weaned away from the dam by gradually introducing them to canned dog food in small portions.

least preferred by owners, even though their dogs seem to like them. A rice-based dry food with a protein source other than beef or organ meat is often recommended for the Dalmatian.

When selecting your dog's diet, three stages of development must be considered: the puppy stage, adult stage and the senior stage.

PUPPY STAGE

Puppies instinctively want to suck milk from their mother's teats, and a normal puppy will exhibit this behavior from just a few moments following birth. If puppies do not attempt to suckle within the first half-hour or so, the breeder should encourage them to do so by placing them on the nipples,

FEEDING TIPS

- Dog food must be served at room temperature, neither too hot nor too cold. Fresh water, changed often and served in a clean bowl, is mandatory, especially when feeding dry food.
- Never feed your dog from the table while you are eating, and never feed your dog leftovers from your own meal. They usually contain too much fat and too much seasoning.
- Dogs must chew their food. Hard pellets are excellent; soups and stews are to be avoided.
- Don't add leftovers or any extras to commercial dog food. The normal food is usually balanced, and adding something extra destroys the balance.
- Except for age-related changes, dogs do not require dietary variations. They can be fed the same diet, day after day, without their becoming bored or ill.

also that of correct quality, fed at suitably frequent intervals, usually every two hours during the first few days of life.

Puppies should be allowed to nurse from their mothers for about the first six weeks, although from the third or fourth week the breeder will begin to introduce small portions of suitable solid food. Most breeders like to introduce alternate milk and meat meals initially, building up to weaning time.

By the time the puppies are seven or a maximum of eight weeks old, they should be fully weaned and fed solely on a proprietary puppy food. Selection of the most suitable, good-quality

Pups are best fed with their mother's milk for the first six weeks, as this provides essential nutrition at a crucial stage of life.

> ## TEST FOR PROPER DIET
> A good test for proper diet is the color, odor, and firmness of your dog's stool. A healthy dog usually produces three semi-hard stools per day. The stools should have no unpleasant odor. They should be the same color from excretion to excretion.

diet at this time is essential, for a puppy's fastest growth rate is during the first year of life. Puppies need protein for proper nutrition during their growth phase, but because of the Dalmatian's stone-forming tendency, the protein source must be carefully chosen. Again, organ meat and beef should be avoided. Something more easily digested, such as lamb in a rice base or a rice-and-vegetable-based food, is better for the Dalmatian. Veterinarians, especially those who have experience dealing with the unique needs of the Dalmatian, are usually able to offer advice in this regard. Breeders are very helpful as well, as they know what has worked in keeping their own dogs stone-free.

The frequency of meals will be reduced over time, as the puppy becomes an adult. Puppy and junior diets should be well balanced for the needs of your dog, so that except in certain circumstances with the advice of your vet, additional vitamins and

A
Worthy
Investment

Veterinary studies have proven that a balanced high-quality diet pays off in your dog's coat quality, behavior and activity level. Invest in premium brands for the maximum benefit for your dog.

minerals will not be required. Feeding "people food" is never advised for the Dalmatian.

ADULT DIETS

A dog is considered an adult when it has stopped growing, so in general the diet of a Dalmatian can be changed to an adult one at about 12 to 15 months of age. Again you should rely upon your veterinarian or dietary specialist to recommend an acceptable maintenance diet. Dog food manufacturers specialize in this type of balanced food, and it is just necessary for you to select the one best suited to your Dal's needs, keeping in mind his unique dietary requirements. Your vet may prefer to recommend a specialized food for your

The Dalmatian's special health concerns require that his diet be carefully monitored. He should only eat what you give him; everything else should be out of his reach.

CHANGE IN DIET

As your Dal's caretaker, you know the importance of keeping his diet consistent, but sometimes when you run out of food or if you're on vacation, you have to make a change quickly. Some dogs will experience digestive problems, but most will not. If you are planning on changing your dog's menu, do so gradually to ensure that your dog will not have any problems. Over a period of four to five days, slowly add the new brand to your dog's existing diet, increasing the percentage of new food each day. Always keep your Dal's health and dietary requirements in mind if varying from his normal food.

Dalmatian, so this will take the confusion out of choosing a food. Also, active dogs may have different requirements than sedate dogs.

SENIOR DIETS

As dogs get older, their metabolism changes. The older dog usually exercises less, moves more slowly and sleeps more. This change in lifestyle and physiological performance requires a change in diet. Since these changes take place slowly, they might not be recognizable. What is easily recognizable is weight gain. By continuing to feed your dog the same amount of adult-maintenance diet when he is slowing

A lactating bitch may need supplementation to her diet. Your veterinarian can help with these special requirements.

down metabolically, your dog will gain weight. Obesity in an older dog compounds the health problems that already accompany old age.

As your dog gets older, few of their organs function up to par. The kidneys slow down and the intestines become less efficient. These age-related factors are best

STORING YOUR FOOD

You must store your dry dog food carefully. Open packages of dog food quickly lose their vitamin value, usually within 90 days of being opened. Mold spores and vermin could also contaminate the food.

handled with a change in diet and a change in feeding schedule to give smaller portions that are more easily digested, thus making it easier for the dog to get maximum nutrition from the food.

There is no single best diet for every older dog. While many dogs do well on light or senior diets, other dogs do better on a lower protein or other special premium diets. Be sensitive to your senior Dalmatian's diet and this will help control other problems that may arise with your old friend.

WATER

Just as your dog needs proper nutrition from his food, water is

Your Dalmatian should always have fresh, clean water from a clean bowl. Some owners offer only distilled water to their Dals.

an essential "nutrient" as well. Water keeps the dog's body properly hydrated and promotes normal function of the body's systems. During housebreaking it is necessary to keep an eye on how much water your Dalmatian is drinking, so that you will be able to anticipate when he will need to relieve himself. Make sure that the dog's water bowl is clean, and elevated, change the water often, making sure that water is always available for your dog.

Water is especially important for the Dalmatian, as it helps to flush his system of urinary crystals. Increased water intake is a major preventative in keeping the dog free of urinary stones and urinary infection. For stone-formers, regular water may not be sufficient and it may be necessary to give affected Dals distilled water only. The word "distilled" is very important; make sure that the water is specified as such. Be careful not to let the Dal gulp water, especially after meals, as this increases the risk of bloat.

Exercising your Dalmatian is extremely important. This Dal is as happy as can be with a big fenced area in which to run and a stick to fetch!

EXERCISE

Exercise is something that cannot be stressed enough with the Dalmatian. Remember that these dogs are capable of traveling long distances on foot and never seem to tire. A Dalmatian without sufficient exercise will become quite hyperactive; it's not good for him physically or mentally. Although the Dalmatian is a very active breed that enjoys exercise, you don't have to be an Olympic athlete to keep up with him. Regular walks, play sessions in the yard or letting the dog run free under your supervision are sufficient forms of exercise for the Dalmatian. For those who are more ambitious, you will find that your Dalmatian, once he is six months of age, also enjoys long walks, hikes or even a swim! Many Dalmatian owners also look to organized competition such as agility to give their dogs an outlet for their energy.

Bear in mind that an overweight dog should never be

suddenly over-exercised; instead, he should be allowed to increase exercise slowly. Not only is exercise essential to keep the dog's body fit, it is essential to his mental well-being. A bored dog will find something to do, which often manifests itself in some type of destructive behavior. In this sense, it is essential for the owner's mental well-being as well!

GROOMING

BRUSHING

Dalmatians shed! Your Dalmatian will need to be groomed regularly, so you should train him to enjoy short grooming sessions from a very early age. Regular brushing will minimize the dead hair's being shed all over your house, furniture and clothes. This will not involve a great deal of time, but ten minutes or so a day should be set aside. It is important that your puppy stands on a solid surface for grooming, a suitable table on which the dog will not slip. Under no circumstances should you leave your Dalmatian alone on a table, for he may all too easily jump off and injure himself.

Routine grooming does not have to be extensive. A thorough once-over with a rubber brush or grooming glove should do the trick. Avoid bristle brushes, as they are not effective in removing dead hair, and avoid wire brushes, which are too abrasive for the

Your Dalmatian will love to go for a hike, but on-lead is the only way to go! Unrestrained exercise is fine in a safely enclosed area, but not in the park or woods.

Dal's skin. As you brush your Dal, take the opportunity to check for any abnormalites or indication of parasites on the skin and coat. By grooming a little each day, or nearly every day, your Dalmatian's coat should never become too problematic and dead hair will be removed as a matter of routine.

GROOMING EQUIPMENT

How much grooming equipment you purchase will depend on how much grooming you are going to do. Here are some basics:

- Rubber brush
- Grooming glove
- Scissors
- Blow dryer
- Rubber mat
- Dog shampoo
- Spray hose attachment
- Towels
- Ear cleaner
- Cotton balls
- Nail clippers

You should brush your Dalmatian regularly. Start acclimating the dog when he is still a puppy and he'll grow to stand politely for his routine grooming.

Your local pet shop will have all kinds of grooming tools. You don't need fancy equipment to keep your Dal looking nice, but brushing is necessary to minimize shedding.

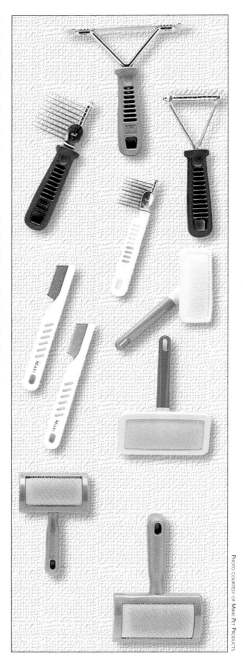

PHOTO COURTESY OF MIKKI PET PRODUCTS.

BATHING

Frequent baths are not recommended for the Dalmatian, as these will dry out his skin, which is already prone to dryness. A dirty patch of coat can easily be cleaned with a wet washcloth, followed by brushing once the coat is dry. However, there are times when your Dal will need a bath. Personally, I always like to stand my dogs on a non-slip mat in the bath tub and then wet the coat thoroughly using a spray attachment. Always test the temperature of the water beforehand so that it is neither too hot nor too cold. Use a mild dog shampoo for sensitive skin, being especially careful of the head. You may want to use only a soapy washcloth on these areas to avoid shampoo's dripping into the dog's eyes and ears. Cotton balls will protect the dog's ears as well, but remember to remove them! Take care to rinse your Dal's coat extremely well. Dry the coat with thick towels, but be prepared—undoubtedly your Dalmatian will want to shake! Finish with a brushing, but only after the coat is dry.

EAR CLEANING

The ears should be kept clean and any excess hair inside the ear should carefully be plucked out. Ears can be cleaned with cotton

> ### SOAP IT UP
> The use of human soap products like shampoo, bubble bath and hand soap can be damaging to a dog's coat and skin. Human products are too strong and remove the protective oils coating the dog's hair and skin (that make him water-resistant). Use only shampoo made especially for dogs. You may like to use a medicated shampoo, which will help to keep external parasites at bay.

balls and a cleaning solution that is specially made for dogs and for this purpose. Be on the lookout for any signs of infection or ear-mite infestation. If your Dalmatian has been shaking his head or

scratching at his ears frequently, this usually indicates a problem. If his ears have an unusual odor, this is a sure sign of mite infestation or infection, and a signal to have his ears checked by the veterinarian.

NAIL CLIPPING

Your Dalmatian should be accustomed to having his nails trimmed at an early age, since it will be part of your maintenance

Dirty patches can be cleaned easily with a wet washcloth, both to keep the white coat clean and to avoid muddy footprints in the house.

A cotton swab can be used to clean the ear, just be careful not to poke or prod into the ear canal.

BATHING BEAUTY

Once you are sure that the dog is thoroughly rinsed, squeeze the excess water out of the coat with your hand and dry him with a heavy towel. You may choose to use a blow dryer on his coat or just let it dry naturally. In cold weather, never allow your dog outside with a wet coat.

There are "dry bath" products on the market, which are sprays and powders intended for spot cleaning that can be used between regular baths, if necessary. They are not substitutes for regular baths, but they are easy to use for touch-ups as they do not require rinsing.

routine throughout his life. Not only does it look nicer, but long nails can scratch someone unintentionally. Also, a long nail has a better chance of ripping and bleeding, or of causing the feet to spread. A good rule of thumb is that if you can hear your dog's

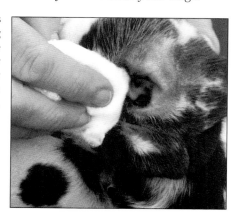

A cotton ball is safe for cleaning in and around the ear. Inspect for ear mites or other abnormalities while you clean.

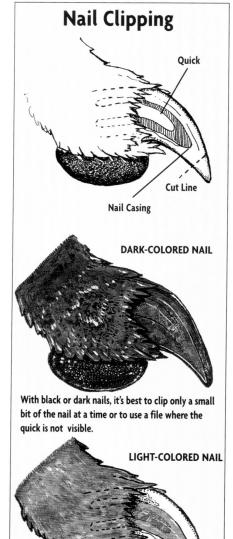

Nail Clipping

Quick

Cut Line

Nail Casing

DARK-COLORED NAIL

With black or dark nails, it's best to clip only a small bit of the nail at a time or to use a file where the quick is not visible.

LIGHT-COLORED NAIL

In light-colored nails, clipping is much simpler because you can see the vein (or quick) that grows inside the casing.

nails clicking on the floor when he walks, his nails are too long.

Before you start cutting, make sure you can identify the "quick" in each nail. The quick is a blood vessel that runs through the center of each nail and grows rather close to the end. It will bleed if accidentally cut, which will be quite painful for the dog as it contains nerve endings. Keep some type of clotting agent on hand, such as a styptic pencil or styptic powder (the type used for shaving). This will stop the bleeding quickly when applied to the end of the cut nail. Do not panic if this happens, just stop the bleeding and talk soothingly to your dog. Once he has calmed down, move on to the next nail. It is better to clip a little at a time.

Hold your pup steady as you begin trimming his nails; you do not want him to make any sudden movements or run away. Talk to him soothingly and stroke him as you clip. Holding his foot in your hand, simply take off the end of each nail in one quick clip. You can purchase nail clippers that are specially made for dogs; you can probably find them wherever you buy pet or grooming supplies.

TRAVELING WITH YOUR DOG

CAR TRAVEL

You should accustom your Dalmatian to riding in a car at an early age. You may or may not

PEDICURE TIP
A dog that spends a lot of time outside on a hard surface, such as cement or pavement, will have his nails naturally worn down and may not need to have them trimmed as often, except maybe in the colder months when he is not outside as much. Regardless, it is best to get your dog accustomed to this procedure at an early age so that he is used to it. Some dogs are especially sensitive about having their feet touched, but if a dog has experienced it since he was young, he should not be bothered by it.

take him in the car often, but at the very least he will need to go to the vet and you do not want these trips to be traumatic for the dog or a big hassle for you. The safest way for a dog to ride in the car is in his crate. If he uses a crate in the house, you can use the same crate for travel.

Put the pup in the crate and

With the "guillotine"-type clipper, you insert the dog's nail and take the tip off in one quick action.

The only safe way to travel with a Dalmatian in your car is when he is safely restrained.

see how he reacts. If he seems uneasy, you can have a passenger hold him on his lap while you drive. Another option is a specially made safety harness for dogs, which straps the dog in much like a seat belt. Do not let the dog roam loose in the vehicle—this is very dangerous! If you should stop short, your dog can be thrown and injured. If the dog starts climbing on you and pestering you while you are driving, you will not be able to concentrate on the road. It is an unsafe situation for everyone—human and canine.

For long trips, be prepared to stop to let the dog relieve himself.

Bring along whatever you need to clean up after him. You should take along some paper kitchen towels and perhaps some old bath towels for use should he have a house-breaking accident in the car or suffer from motion sickness.

AIR TRAVEL

While it is possible to take a dog on a flight, special arrangements must be made ahead of time. The dog will be required to travel in a fiberglass crate and you should always check in advance with the airline regarding specific requirements. To help the dog be at ease, put one of his favorite toys in the

Never drive with your dog free in the car. It is dangerous for all involved.

crate with him. Do not feed the dog for several hours before the trip to minimize his need to relieve himself.

Make sure that your dog is properly identified and that your contact information appears on his ID tags and on his crate. Animals travel in a different area of the plane than human passengers, so every rule must be strictly followed so as to prevent the risk of getting separated from your dog.

TRAVELING SAFELY

The most extensive travel you do with your dog may be limited to trips to the veterinarian's office—or you may decide to bring him along for long distances when the family goes on vacation. Whichever the case, it is important to consider your dog's safety while traveling.

Accustom the pup to travel in his crate. A few of his favorite toys will help him feel more comfortable during the trip.

VACATIONS AND BOARDING

So you want to take your family vacation—and you want to include *all* members of the family. You would probably make arrangements for accommodations ahead of time anyway, but this is especially important when traveling with a dog. You do not want to make an overnight stop at the only place around for miles and find out that they do not allow dogs. Also, you do not want to reserve a place for your family without confirming that you are traveling with a dog, because if it is against their policy you may not have a place to stay.

Alternatively, if you are traveling and choose not to bring your Dalmatian, you will have to make arrangements for him while you are away. Some options are to take him to a neighbor's house to stay while you are gone, to have a trusted neighbor stop by often or stay at your house or to bring your dog to a reputable boarding kennel. If you choose to board him at a kennel, you should visit in advance to see the facility, how clean it is and where the dogs are kept. Talk to some of the employees and see how they treat the dogs—do they spend time with the dogs, play with them, exercise them, etc.? Also find out the kennel's policy on vaccinations and what they require. This is for all of the dogs' safety, since when dogs are kept together, there is a greater risk of diseases being passed from dog to dog.

TRAVELING ABROAD

For international travel you will have to make arrangements well in advance (perhaps months), as countries' regulations pertaining to bringing in animals differ. There may be special health certificates and/or vaccinations that your dog will need before taking the trip; sometimes this has to be done within a certain time frame. In rabies-free countries, you will need to bring proof of the dog's rabies vaccination and there may be a quarantine period upon arrival.

IDENTIFICATION

Your Dalmatian is your valued companion and friend. That is why you always keep a close eye on him and you have made sure that he cannot escape from the yard or wriggle out of his collar and run away from you. However, accidents can happen and there may come a time when your dog unexpectedly gets separated from you. If this unfortunate event should occur, the first thing on your mind will be finding him. Proper identification, including an ID tag, a tattoo and possibly a microchip, will increase the chances of his being returned to you safely and quickly.

No matter how long or short the trip, your Dalmatian will be safe in the comfort of his crate.

Should you find it necessary to board your dog while you are on vacation, or are unable to care for the dog for any reason, ask your vet to recommend a local boarding kennel. Be sure that the kennel is clean, with an educated and attentive staff.

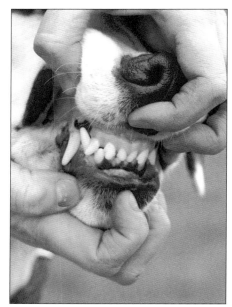

You should clean your Dalmatian's teeth at home in between veterinary visits. Always inspect the teeth and gums for the accumulation of plaque or any other foreign matter.

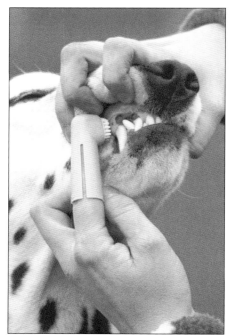

A short fence is no match for a Dalmatian on the go! To prevent an escape, make sure that the yard is securely fenced. Proper identification is also essential—if your Dal should get out of the yard you want to ensure his safe return.

COLLAR REQUIRED

If your dog gets lost, he is not able to ask for directions home. Identification tags fastened to the collar give important information—the dog's name, the owner's name, the owner's address and a telephone number where the owner can be reached. This makes it easy for whomever finds the dog to contact the owner and arrange to have the dog returned. An added advantage is that a person will be more likely to approach a lost dog who has ID tags on his collar; it tells the person that this is somebody's pet rather than a stray. This is the easiest and fastest method of identification, provided that the tags stay on the collar and the collar stays on the dog.

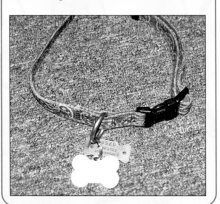

TRAINING YOUR
DALMATIAN

Living with an untrained dog is a lot like owning a piano that you do not know how to play—it is a nice object to look at, but it does not do much more than that to bring you pleasure. Now try taking piano lessons, and suddenly the piano comes alive and brings forth magical sounds and rhythms that set your heart singing and your body swaying.

The same is true with your Dalmatian. Any dog is a big responsibility and, if not trained sensibly, may develop unaccept-able behavior that annoys you or could even cause family friction.

To train your Dalmatian, you may like to enroll in an obedience class. Teach him good manners as you learn how and why he behaves the way he does. Find out

how to communicate with your dog and how to recognize and understand his communications with you. Suddenly the dog takes on a new role in your life—he is smart, interesting, well behaved and fun to be with. He demonstrates his bond of devotion to you daily. In other words, your Dalmatian does wonders for your ego because he constantly reminds you that you are not only his leader, you are his hero!

Those involved with teaching dog obedience and counseling owners about their dogs' behavior

HONOR AND OBEY

Dogs are the most honorable animals in existence. They consider another species (humans) as their own. They interface with you. You are their leader. Puppies perceive children to be on their level; their actions around small children are different from their behavior around their adult masters.

FEAR AGGRESSION

Pups who are subjected to physical abuse during training commonly end up with behavioral problems as adults. One common result of abuse is fear aggression, in which a dog will lash out, bare his teeth, snarl and finally bite someone by whom he feels threatened. For example, your daughter may be playing with the dog one afternoon. As they play hide-and-seek, she backs the dog into a corner and, as she attempts to tease him playfully, he bites her hand. Examine the cause of this behavior. Did your daughter ever hit the dog? Did someone who resembles your daughter hit or scream at the dog?

Fortunately, fear aggression is relatively easy to correct. Have your daughter engage in only positive activities with the dog, such as feeding, petting and walking. She should not give any corrections or negative feedback. If the dog still growls or cowers away from her, allow someone else to accompany them. After approximately one week, the dog should feel that he can rely on her for many positive things, and he will also be prevented from reacting fearfully towards anyone who might resemble her.

have discovered some interesting facts about dog ownership. For example, training dogs when they are puppies results in the highest rate of success in developing well-mannered and well-adjusted adult dogs. Training an older dog, from six months to six years of age, can produce almost equal results, providing that the owner accepts the dog's slower rate of learning capability and is willing to work patiently to help the dog succeed at developing to his fullest potential. Unfortunately, many owners of untrained adult dogs lack the patience factor, so they do not persist until their dogs are successful at learning particular behaviors.

Training a puppy aged 10 to 16 weeks (20 weeks at the most) is like working with a dry sponge in a pool of water. The pup soaks up whatever you show him and constantly looks for more things to do and learn. At this early age, his body is not yet producing hormones, and therein lies the reason for such a high rate of success. Without hormones, he is focused on his owners and not particularly interested in investigating other places, dogs, people, etc. You are his leader: his provider of food, water, shelter and security. He latches onto you and wants to stay close. He will usually follow you from room to room, will not let you out of his sight when you are outdoors with him

Curious and clever, this young Dalmatian is ready to explore the world! There's no better time to start his education than now!

THINK BEFORE YOU BARK

Dogs are sensitive to their masters' moods and emotions. Use your voice wisely when communicating with your dog. Never raise your voice at your dog unless you are trying to correct him. "Barking" at your dog can become as meaningless as "dogspeak" is to you.

and will respond in like manner to the people and animals you encounter. If you greet a friend warmly, he will be happy to greet the person as well. If, however, you are hesitant or anxious about the approach of a stranger, he will respond accordingly.

Once the puppy begins to produce hormones, his natural

behaviors are the same. After all, no dog, whether puppy or adult, likes harsh or inhumane methods. All creatures, however, respond favorably to gentle motivational methods and sincere praise and encouragement. Dalmatians particularly seem to respond to positive reinforcement in training. Now let us get started.

Be a good citizen. Clean up after your dog no matter where he relieves himself. Your pet shop will have many gadgets to make the task simpler.

curiosity emerges and he begins to investigate the world around him. It is at this time when you may notice that the untrained dog begins to wander away from you and even ignore your commands to stay close. When this behavior becomes a problem, the owner has two choices: get rid of the dog or train him. It is strongly urged that you choose the latter option.

There are usually classes within a reasonable distance from your home, but you also do a lot to train your dog yourself. Sometimes there are classes available, but the tuition is costly. Whatever the circumstances, the methods of training your dog at home lie within the pages of this book.

This chapter is devoted to helping you train your Dalmatian at home. If the recommended procedures are followed faithfully, you may expect positive results that will prove rewarding to both you and your dog.

Whether your new charge is a puppy or a mature adult, the methods of teaching and the techniques we use in training basic

HOUSEBREAKING

You can train a puppy to relieve itself wherever you choose, but the area must be somewhere suitable. You should bear in mind from the outset that when your puppy is old enough to go out in public places, any canine deposits must be removed at once. You will always have to carry with you a small plastic bag or "poop-scoop."

Outdoor training includes such surfaces as grass, dirt and cement. Indoor training usually means training your dog to newspaper, but this is not a feasible option with a dog the size of the Dalmatian.

When deciding on the surface

TRAINING TIP
Training a dog is a life experience. Many parents admit that much of what they know about raising children they learned from caring for their dogs. Dogs respond to love, fairness and guidance, just as children do. Become a good dog owner and you may become an even better parent.

> **HOW MANY TIMES A DAY?**
>
> | AGE | RELIEF TRIPS |
> |---|---|
> | To 14 weeks | 10 |
> | 14–22 weeks | 8 |
> | 22–32 weeks | 6 |
> | Adulthood | 4 |
> | (dog stops growing) | |
>
> These are estimates, of course, but they are a guide to the *minimum* number of opportunities a dog should have each day to relieve himself.

after he has been sleeping and any time he indicates that he is looking for a place to urinate or defecate. The urinary and intestinal tract muscles of very young puppies are not fully developed. Therefore, like human babies, puppies need to relieve themselves frequently.

Take your puppy out often— every hour for an eight-week-old, for example, and always immediately after sleeping and eating. The older the puppy, the less often he will need to relieve himself.

A Dalmatan who is socialized and trained will be adaptable to any situation, however unfamiliar.

and location that you will want your Dalmatian to use, be sure it is going to be permanent. Training your dog to grass and then changing your mind two months later is extremely difficult for both dog and owner.

Next, choose the command you will use each and every time you want your puppy to void. "Hurry up" and "Go make" are examples of commands commonly used by dog owners. Get in the habit of giving the puppy your chosen relief command before you take him out. That way, when he becomes an adult, you will be able to determine if he wants to go out when you ask him. A confirmation will be signs of interest, wagging his tail, watching you intently, going to the door, etc.

PUPPY'S NEEDS
A puppy needs to relieve himself after play periods, after each meal,

Finally, as a mature healthy adult, he will require only three to five relief trips per day.

HOUSING

Since the types of housing and control you provide for your puppy have a direct relationship on the success of housebreaking, we consider the various aspects of both before we begin training. Bringing a new puppy home and turning him loose in your house can be compared to turning a child loose in a sports arena and telling the child that the place is all his! The sheer enormity of the place would be too much for him to handle.

Instead, offer the puppy clearly defined areas where he can play, sleep, eat and live. A room of the house where the family gathers is the most obvious choice. Puppies are social animals and need to feel a part of the pack right from the start. Hearing your voice, watching you while you are doing things and smelling you nearby are all positive reinforcers that he is now a member of your pack. Usually a family room, the kitchen or a nearby adjoining breakfast area is ideal for providing safety and security for both puppy and owner.

Within that room, there should be a smaller area that the puppy can call his own. An alcove, a wire or fiberglass dog crate or a fenced (not boarded!) corner from which he can view the activities of his new family will be fine. The size of the area or crate is the key factor here. The area must be large enough for the puppy to lie down and stretch out as well as stand up without rubbing his head on the top, yet small enough so that he cannot relieve himself at one end and sleep at the other without coming into contact with his droppings before he is fully trained to relieve himself outside.

Dogs are, by nature, clean animals and will not remain close to their relief areas unless forced to do so. In those cases, they then become dirty dogs and usually remain that way for life.

The designated area should be lined with clean bedding and a toy. Water must always be available, in a non-spill container.

CONTROL

By control, we mean helping the puppy to create a lifestyle pattern

---

TRAINING RULES

If you want to be successful in training your dog, you have four rules to obey yourself:

1. Develop an understanding of how a dog thinks.
2. Do not blame the dog for lack of communication.
3. Define your dog's personality and act accordingly.
4. Have patience and be consistent.

A crate may be the most useful tool in caring for your dog. This young litter enjoys the sunshine from the safety of a wire crate.

that will be compatible to that of his human pack (you!). Just as we guide little children to learn our way of life, we must show the puppy when it is time to play, eat, sleep, exercise and even entertain himself.

Your puppy should always sleep in his crate. He should also learn that, during times of household confusion and excessive human activity such as at breakfast when family members are preparing for the day, he can play by himself in relative safety and comfort in his designated area. Each time you leave the puppy alone, he should understand exactly where he is to stay. Puppies are chewers. They cannot tell the difference between lamp cords, television wires, shoes, table legs, etc. Chewing into a television wire, for example, can be fatal to the puppy, while a shorted wire can start a fire in the house.

If the puppy chews on the

arm of the chair when he is alone, you will probably discipline him angrily when you get home. Thus, he makes the association that your coming home means he is going to be punished. (He will not remember chewing up the chair and is incapable of making the association of the discipline with his naughty deed.)

Other times of excitement, such as family parties, etc., can be fun for the puppy, provided he can view the activities from the security of his designated area. He is not underfoot and he is not being fed all sorts of treats that will probably cause him stomach distress, yet he still feels a part of the fun.

SCHEDULE

A puppy should be taken to his relief area each time he is released from his designated area, after meals, after a play session, when

---

THE GOLDEN RULE

The golden rule of dog training is simple. For each "question" (command), there is only one correct answer (reaction). One command = one reaction. Keep practicing the command until the dog reacts correctly without hesitating. Be repetitive but not monotonous. Dogs get bored just as people do!

CANINE DEVELOPMENT SCHEDULE

It is important to understand how and at what age a puppy develops into adulthood.
If you are a puppy owner, consult the following Canine Development Schedule to
determine the stage of development your puppy is currently experiencing.
This knowledge will help you as you work with the puppy in the weeks and months ahead.

Period	Age	Characteristics
FIRST TO THIRD	BIRTH TO SEVEN WEEKS	Puppy needs food, sleep and warmth, and responds to simple and gentle touching. Needs mother for security and disciplining. Needs littermates for learning and interacting with other dogs. Pup learns to function within a pack and learns pack order of dominance. Begin socializing pup with adults and children for short periods. Pup begins to become aware of his environment.
FOURTH	EIGHT TO TWELVE WEEKS	Brain is fully developed. Pup needs socializing with outside world. Remove from mother and littermates. Needs to change from canine pack to human pack. Human dominance necessary. Fear period occurs between 8 and 12 weeks. Avoid fright and pain.
FIFTH	THIRTEEN TO SIXTEEN WEEKS	Training and formal obedience should begin. Less association with other dogs, more with people, places, situations. Period will pass easily if you remember this is pup's change-to-adolescence time. Be firm and fair. Flight instinct prominent. Permissiveness and over-disciplining can do permanent damage. Praise for good behavior.
JUVENILE	FOUR TO EIGHT MONTHS	Another fear period about 7 to 8 months of age. It passes quickly, but be cautious of fright and pain. Sexual maturity reached. Dominant traits established. Dog should understand sit, down, come and stay by now.

NOTE: THESE ARE APPROXIMATE TIME FRAMES. ALLOW FOR INDIVIDUAL DIFFERENCES IN PUPPIES.

he first wakes up in the morning (at age eight weeks, this can mean 5 a.m.!). The puppy will indicate that he's ready "to go" by circling or sniffing busily—do not misinterpret these signs. For a puppy less than ten weeks of age, a routine of taking him out every hour is necessary. As the puppy grows, he will be able to wait for longer periods of time.

Keep trips to his relief area short. Stay no more than five or six minutes and then return to the house. If he goes during that time, praise him lavishly and take him indoors immediately. If he does not, but he has an accident when you go back indoors, pick him up immediately, say "No! No!" and return to his relief area. Wait a

BE CONSISTENT

Most of all, be consistent. Always take your dog to the same location, always use the same command, and always have him on lead when he is in his relief area, unless a fenced-in yard is available.

By following the Success Method, your puppy will be completely housebroken by the time his muscle and brain development reach maturity. Keep in mind that small breeds usually mature faster than large breeds, but all puppies should be trained by six months of age.

few minutes, then return to the house again. Never hit a puppy or rub his face in urine or excrement when he has an accident!

Once indoors, put the puppy in his crate until you have had time to clean up his accident. Then release him to the family area and watch him more closely than before. Chances are, his accident was a result of your not picking up his signal or waiting too long before offering him the opportunity to relieve himself. Never hold a grudge against the puppy for accidents.

Let the puppy learn that going outdoors means it is time to relieve himself, not play. Once trained, he will be able to play indoors and out and still differentiate between the times for play versus the times for relief.

Help him develop regular hours for naps, being alone, playing by himself and just resting, all in his crate. Encourage him to entertain himself while you are busy with your activities. Let him learn that having you near is comforting, but it is not your main purpose in life to provide him with undivided attention.

Each time you put a puppy in his own area, use the same command, whatever suits best. Soon, he will run to his crate or special area when he hears you say those words.

Crate training provides safety for you, the puppy and the home.

The crate you buy should be of ample size for a full-grown Dalmatian. Once your Dal is housebroken, you can offer water in the crate.

It also provides the puppy with a feeling of security, and that helps the puppy achieve self-confidence and clean habits.

Remember that one of the primary ingredients in housebreaking your puppy is control. Regardless of your lifestyle, there will always be occasions when you will need to have a place where your dog can stay and be happy and safe. Training is the answer for now and in the future.

In conclusion, a few key elements are really all you need for a successful housebreaking method—consistency, frequency, praise, control and supervision. By following these procedures with a normal, healthy puppy, you and the puppy will soon be past the stage of accidents and ready to move on to a full and rewarding life together.

ROLES OF DISCIPLINE, REWARD AND PUNISHMENT

Discipline, training one to act in accordance with rules, brings order to life. It is as simple as that. Without discipline, particularly in a group society, chaos reigns supreme and the group will eventually perish. Humans and canines are social animals and need some form of discipline in order to function effectively. They must procure food, protect their home base and their young and reproduce to keep the species going. If there were no discipline in the lives of social animals, they would eventually die from starvation and/or predation by other stronger animals. In the case of domestic canines, dogs need discipline in their lives in order to understand how their pack (you and other family members) functions and how they must act in order to survive.

A large humane society in a highly populated area recently

THE CLEAN LIFE

By providing sleeping and resting quarters that fit the dog, and offering frequent opportunities to relieve himself outside his quarters, the puppy quickly learns that the outdoors (or the newspaper if you are training him to paper) is the place to go when he needs to urinate or defecate. It also reinforces his innate desire to keep his sleeping quarters clean. This, in turn, helps develop the muscle control that will eventually produce a dog with clean living habits.

surveyed dog owners regarding their satisfaction with their relationships with their dogs. People who had trained their dogs were 75% more satisfied with their pets than those who had never trained their dogs.

Dr. Edward Thorndike, a noted psychologist, established *Thorndike's Theory of Learning*, which states that a behavior that results in a pleasant event tends to be repeated. A behavior that results in an unpleasant event tends not to be repeated. It is this theory on which training

THE SUCCESS METHOD

Success that comes by luck is usually short-lived. Success that comes by well-thought-out proven methods is often more easily achieved and permanent. This is the Success Method. It is designed to give you, the puppy owner, a simple yet proven way to help your puppy develop clean living habits and a feeling of security in his new environment.

6 Steps to Successful Crate Training

1 Tell the puppy "Crate time!" and place him in the crate with a small treat (a piece of cheese or half of a biscuit). Let him stay in the crate for five minutes while you are in the same room. Then release him and praise lavishly. Never release him when he is fussing. Wait until he is quiet before you let him out.

2 Repeat Step 1 several times a day.

3 The next day, place the puppy in the crate as before. Let him stay there for ten minutes. Do this several times.

4 Continue building time in five-minute increments until the puppy stays in his crate for 30 minutes with you in the room. Always take him to his relief area after prolonged periods in his crate.

5 Now go back to Step 1 and let the puppy stay in his crate for five minutes, this time while you are out of the room.

6 Once again, build crate time in five-minute increments with you out of the room. When the puppy will stay willingly in his crate (he may even fall asleep!) for 30 minutes with you out of the room, he will be ready to stay in it for several hours at a time.

methods are based today. For example, if you manipulate a dog to perform a specific behavior and reward him for doing it, he is likely to do it again because he enjoyed the end result.

Occasionally, punishment, a penalty inflicted for an offense, is necessary. The best type of punishment often comes from an outside source. For example, a child is told not to touch the stove because he may get burned. He disobeys and touches the stove. In doing so, he receives a burn. From that time on, he respects the heat of the stove and avoids contact with it. Therefore, a behavior that results in an unpleasant event tends not to be repeated.

A good example of a dog's learning the hard way is the dog who chases the house cat. He is told many times to leave the cat alone, yet he persists in teasing the cat. Then, one day he begins chasing the cat but the cat turns and swipes a claw across the dog's face, leaving him with a painful gash on his nose. The final result is that the dog stops chasing the cat.

ATTENTION!

Your dog is actually training you at the same time you are training him. Dogs do things to get attention. They usually repeat whatever succeeds in getting your attention.

TRAINING EQUIPMENT

COLLAR AND LEAD

For a Dalmatian, the collar and lead that you use for training must be one with which you are easily able to work, not too heavy for the dog and perfectly safe.

TREATS

Have a bag of treats on hand. Something nutritious (low-purine, of course) and easy to swallow works best. Use a soft

Offer a treat as you gently guide the dog into the proper position. Sit is a simple command that can be taught easily with some practice and the help of a few treats.

"School" should capture the dog's attention and heighten his expectations that something really fun and interesting is coming...and maybe a tasty treat, too.

PLAN TO PLAY

The puppy should have regular play and exercise sessions when he is with you or a family member. Exercise for a very young puppy can consist of a short walk around the house or yard. Playing can include fetching games with a large ball or a special toy. (All puppies teethe and need soft things upon which to chew.) Remember to restrict play periods to indoors within his living area (the family room, for example) until he is completely housebroken.

PRACTICE MAKES PERFECT!

- Have training lessons with your dog every day in several short segments—three to five times a day for a few minutes at a time is ideal.
- Do not have long practice sessions. The dog will become easily bored.
- Never practice when you are tired, ill, worried or in an otherwise negative mood. This will transmit to the dog and may have an adverse effect on his performance.

   Think fun, short and above all *positive!* End each session on a high note, rather than a failed exercise, and make sure to give a lot of praise. Enjoy the training and help your dog enjoy it, too.

treat, rather than a dry biscuit. By the time the dog gets done chewing a dry treat, he will forget why he is being rewarded in the first place! Using food rewards will not teach a dog to beg at the table—the only way to teach a dog to beg at the table is to give him food from the table. In training, rewarding the dog with a food treat will help him associate praise and the treats with learning new behaviors that obviously please his owner.

TRAINING BEGINS: ASK THE DOG A QUESTION

In order to teach your dog anything, you must first get his attention. After all, he cannot learn anything if he is looking away from you with his mind on something else.

   To get his attention, ask him, "School?" and immediately walk over to him and give him a treat as you tell him "Good dog." Wait a minute or two and repeat the routine, this time with a treat in your hand as you approach within a foot of the dog. Do not go directly to him, but stop about a foot short of him and hold out the treat as you ask, "School?" He will see you approaching with a treat in your hand and most likely begin walking toward you. As you meet, give him the treat and praise again.

   The third time, ask the question, have a treat in your hand and walk only a short distance toward the dog so that he must walk almost all the way to you. As he reaches you, give him the treat and praise again.

   By this time, the dog will

Dalmatians, like all dogs, want and need proper training and discipline, and they look to their owners to provide it.

You can use hand signals as well as voice commands to get your Dal's attention and teach commands.

THE BASIC COMMANDS

TEACHING SIT

Now that you have the dog's attention, attach his lead and hold it in your left hand and a food treat in your right. Place your food hand at the dog's nose and let him lick the treat but not take it from you. Say "Sit" and slowly raise your food hand from in front of the dog's nose up over his head so that he is looking at the ceiling. As he bends his head upward, he will have to bend his knees to maintain his balance. As he bends his knees, he will assume a sit position. At that point, release the food treat and praise lavishly with comments such as "Good dog! Good sit!", etc. Remember to always praise enthusiastically, because dogs relish verbal praise from their owners and feel so proud of themselves whenever they accomplish a behavior.

You will not use food forever

probably be getting the idea that if he pays attention to you, especially when you ask that question, it will pay off in treats and fun activities for him. In other words, he learns that "school" means doing fun things with you that result in treats and positive attention for him.

Remember that the dog does not understand your verbal language, he only recognizes sounds. Your question translates to a series of sounds for him, and those sounds become the signal to go to you and pay attention; if he does, he will get to interact with you plus receive treats and praise.

REAP THE REWARDS

If you start with a normal, healthy dog and give him time, patience and some carefully executed lessons, you will reap the rewards of that training for the life of the dog. And what a life it will be! The two of you will find immeasurable pleasure in the companionship you have built together with love, respect and understanding. Good luck and enjoy!

in getting the dog to obey your commands. Food is only used to teach new behaviors, and once the dog knows what you want when you give a specific command, you will wean him off the food treats but still maintain the verbal praise. After all, you will always have your voice with you, but there will be many times when you have no food rewards but expect the dog to obey.

TEACHING DOWN

Teaching the down exercise is easy when you understand how the dog perceives the down position, and it is very difficult when you do not. Dogs perceive the down position as a submissive one; therefore, teaching the down exercise using a forceful method can sometimes make the dog develop such a fear of the down that he either runs away when you say "Down" or he attempts to snap at the person who tries to force him down.

Have the dog sit close alongside your left leg, facing in the same direction as you are. Hold the lead in your left hand and a food treat in your right. Now place your left hand lightly on the top of the dog's shoulders where they meet above the spinal cord. Do not push down on the dog's shoulders; simply rest your left hand there so you can guide the dog to lie down close to your left leg rather than to swing away from your side when he drops.

Now place the food hand at the dog's nose, say "Down" very softly (almost a whisper), and slowly lower the food hand to the dog's front feet. When the food hand reaches the floor, begin moving it forward along the floor in front of the dog. Keep talking softly to the dog, saying things like, "Do you want this treat? You can do this, good dog." Your reassuring tone of voice will help calm the dog as he tries to follow the food hand in order to get the treat.

Using a treat makes the down exercise much easier to introduce.

After your dog has mastered the sit, you can progress to more advanced commands like the sit/stay.

You can easily train your dog to stay in the down position once he has learned the down command.

When the dog's elbows touch the floor, release the food and praise softly. Try to get the dog to maintain the down position for several seconds before you let him sit up again. The goal here is to get the dog to settle down and not feel threatened in the down position.

TEACHING STAY

It is easy to teach the dog to stay in either a sit or a down position. Again, we use food and praise during the teaching process as we help the dog to understand exactly what it is that we are expecting him to do.

To teach the sit/stay, start with the dog sitting on your left side as before and hold the lead in your left hand. Have a food treat in your

right hand and place your food hand at the dog's nose. Say "Stay" and step out on your right foot to stand directly in front of the dog,

A BORN PRODIGY

Occasionally, a dog and owner who have not attended formal classes have been able to earn entry-level obedience titles by obtaining competition rules and regulations from a local kennel club and practicing on their own to a degree of perfection. Obtaining the higher level titles, however, almost always requires extensive training under the tutelage of experienced instructors. In addition, the more difficult levels require more specialized equipment whereas the lower levels do not.

No matter which command you are teaching, keeping the dog's focus on the lesson is essential.

toe to toe, as he licks and nibbles the treat. Be sure to keep his head facing upward to maintain the sit position. Count to five and then swing around to stand next to the dog again with him on your left. As soon as you get back to the original position, release the food and praise lavishly.

To teach the down/stay, do the down as previously described. As soon as the dog lies down, say "Stay" and step out on your right foot just as you did in the sit/stay. Count to five and then return to stand beside the dog with him on your left side. Release the treat and praise as always.

Within a week or ten days, you can begin to add a bit of distance between you and your

"WHERE ARE YOU?"
When calling the dog, do not say "Come." Say things like, "Rover, where are you? See if you can find me! I have a biscuit for you!" Keep up a constant line of chatter with coaxing sounds and frequent questions such as, "Where are you?" The dog will learn to follow the sound of your voice to locate you and receive his reward.

dog when you leave him. When you do, use your left hand open with the palm facing the dog as a stay signal, much the same as the hand signal a police officer uses to stop traffic at an intersection. Hold the food treat in your right hand as before, but this time the food is not touching the dog's nose. He will watch the food hand and quickly learn that he is going to get that treat as soon as you return to his side.

When you can stand 1 yard away from your dog for 30 seconds, you can then begin building time and distance in both stays. Eventually, the dog can be expected to remain in the stay position for prolonged periods of time until you return to him or call him to you. Always praise lavishly when he stays.

TEACHING COME

If you make teaching "come" a fun experience, you should never have a "student" that does not love the game or that fails to come when called. The secret, it seems, is never to teach the word "come."

At times when an owner most wants his dog to come when called, the owner is likely upset or anxious and he allows these feelings to come through in the tone of his voice when he calls his dog. Hearing that desperation in his owner's voice, the dog fears the results of going to him and therefore either disobeys outright or runs in the opposite direction. The secret, therefore, is to teach the dog a game and, when you want him to come to you, simply play the game. It is practically a no-fail solution!

To begin, have several members of your family take a few food treats and each go into a different room in the house. Take turns calling the dog, and each person should celebrate the dog's finding him with a treat and lots of happy praise. When a person calls the dog, he is actually inviting the dog to find him and get a treat as a reward for "winning."

Playing "fetch" games with your Dalmatian and praising him upon his return to you will help positively reinforce the come command.

The heel command is an absolute requirement for a well-behaved dog. You do not want him pulling ahead or lagging behind as you walk with him.

old companion dog who went blind, but who never fails to locate her owner when asked, "Where are you?"

Children particularly love to play this game with their dogs. Children can hide in smaller places like a shower or bathtub, behind a bed or under a table. The dog needs to work a little bit harder to find these hiding places, but when he does he loves to celebrate with a treat and a tussle with a favorite youngster.

TEACHING HEEL
Heeling means that the dog walks beside the owner without pulling.

When you stop walking, the dog should immediately assume the sit position by your left side.

A few turns of the "Where are you?" game and the dog will figure out that everyone is playing the game and that each person has a big celebration awaiting his success at locating them. Once he learns to love the game, simply calling out "Where are you?" will bring him running from wherever he is when he hears that all-important question.

The come command is recognized as one of the most important things to teach a dog, but there are trainers who work with thousands of dogs and never teach the actual word "come." Yet these dogs will race to respond to a person who uses the dog's name followed by "Where are you?" For example, a woman has a 12-year-

It takes time and patience on the owner's part to succeed at teaching the dog that he (the owner) will not proceed unless the dog is walking calmly beside him. Pulling out ahead on the lead is definitely not acceptable.

Begin with holding the lead in your left hand as the dog sits beside your left leg. Move the loop end of the lead to your right hand but keep your left hand short on the lead so it keeps the dog in close next to you.

Say "Heel" and step forward on your left foot. Keep the dog close to you and take three steps. Stop and have the dog sit next to you in what we now call the "heel position." Praise verbally, but do not touch the dog. Hesitate a moment and begin again with "Heel," taking three steps and stopping, at which point the dog is told to sit again.

Your goal here is to have the dog walk those three steps without pulling on the lead. When he will walk calmly beside you for three steps without pulling, increase the number of steps you take to five. When he will walk politely beside you while you take five steps, you can increase the length of your walk to ten steps. Keep increasing the length of your stroll until the dog will walk quietly beside you without pulling as long as you want him to heel. When you stop heeling,

Your dog should be well trained in the heel exercise and be able to comfortably keep pace by your side as you walk.

indicate to the dog that the exercise is over by verbally praising as you pet him and say "OK, good dog." The "OK" is used as a release word, meaning that the exercise is finished and the dog is free to relax.

If you are dealing with a dog who insists on pulling you around, simply "put on your brakes" and stand your ground until the dog realizes that the two of you are not going anywhere

TUG OF WALK?

If you begin teaching the heel by taking long walks and letting the dog pull you along, he misinterprets this action as an acceptable form of taking a walk. When you pull back on the leash to counteract his pulling, he reads that tug as a signal to pull even harder!

HEELING WELL

Teach your dog to heel in an enclosed area. Once you think the dog will obey reliably and you want to attempt advanced obedience exercises such as off-lead heeling, test him in a fenced-in area so he cannot run away.

until he is beside you and moving at your pace, not his. It may take some time just standing there to convince the dog that you are the leader and you will be the one to decide on the direction and speed of your travel.

Each time the dog looks up at you or slows down to give a slack lead between the two of you, quietly praise him and say, "Good heel. Good dog." Eventually, the dog will begin to respond and within a few days he will be walking politely beside you without pulling on the lead. At first, the training sessions should be kept short and very positive; soon the dog will be able to walk nicely with you for increasingly longer distances. Remember also to give the dog free time and the opportunity to run and play when you are done with heel practice.

WEANING OFF FOOD IN TRAINING

Food is used in training new behaviors. Once the dog understands what behavior goes with a specific command, it is

You never know what your Dalmatian will do to earn a treat!

time to start weaning him off the food treats. At first, give a treat after each exercise. Then, start to give a treat only after every other exercise. Mix up the times when you offer a food reward and the times when you only offer praise so that the dog will never know when he is going to receive both food and praise and when he is going to receive only praise. This is called a variable ratio reward system and it proves successful because there is always the chance that the owner will produce a treat, so the dog never stops trying for that reward. No matter what, *always* give verbal praise.

OBEDIENCE CLASSES

It is a good idea to enroll in an obedience class if one is available in your area. If yours is a show dog, showing classes would be more appropriate. Many areas have dog clubs that offer basic obedience training as well as preparatory

OBEDIENCE CLASS
A basic obedience beginner's class usually lasts for six to eight weeks. Dog and owner attend an hour-long lesson once a week and practice for a few minutes, several times a day, each day at home. If done properly, the whole procedure will result in a well-mannered dog and an owner who delights in living with a pet that is eager to please and enjoys doing things with his owner.

classes for obedience competition. There are also local dog trainers who offer similar classes.

At obedience trials, dogs can earn titles at various levels of competition. The beginning levels of competition include basic behaviors such as sit, down, heel, etc. The more advanced levels of competition include jumping, retrieving, scent discrimination and signal work. The advanced levels require a dog and owner to put a lot of time and effort into their training, and the titles that can be earned at these levels of competition are very prestigious.

OTHER ACTIVITIES FOR LIFE
Whether a dog is trained in the structured environment of a class or alone with his owner at home, there are many activities that can bring fun and rewards to both owner and dog once they have

mastered basic control.

Teaching the dog to help out around the home, in the yard or on the farm provides great satisfaction to both dog and owner. In addition, the dog's help makes life a little easier for his owner and raises his stature as a valued companion to his family. It helps give the dog a purpose by occupying his mind and providing an outlet for his energy.

Hiking is an exciting and healthy activity that the dog can be taught without assistance from more than his owner. Dalmatians seem to really enjoy this activity and are very well suited to it. The exercise of walking and climbing is good for man and dog alike, and the bond that they develop together is priceless.

If you are interested in participating in organized competition with your Dalmatian, there are activities other than obedience in which you and your dog can become involved. Agility is a popular and fun sport where dogs run through an obstacle course that includes various jumps, tunnels and other exercises to test the dog's speed and coordination. The owners run through the course beside their dogs to give commands and to guide them through the course. Although competitive, the focus is on fun: it's fun to do, fun to watch and a wonderful form of exercise, and Dalmatians excel at it.

Dogs suffer from many of the same physical illnesses as people. They might even share many of the same psychological problems. Since people usually know more about human diseases than canine maladies, many of the terms used in this chapter will be familiar but not necessarily those used by veterinarians. We will use the term *x-ray*, instead of the more acceptable term radiograph. We will also use the familiar term *symptoms* even though dogs don't have symptoms, which are verbal descriptions of the patient's feelings. Dogs instead have *clinical signs*. Since dogs can't speak, we have to look for clinical signs...but we still use the term *symptoms* in this book.

As a general rule, medicine is *practiced*. That term is not

> ### EARLY DETECTION
> Any dog can be born with dysplastic problems. Your vet can usually diagnose the potential or actual problem using x-rays. If caught early enough, dysplasia can be corrected.

arbitrary. Medicine is a constantly changing art as we learn more and more about genetics, electronic aids (like CAT scans) and daily laboratory advances. There are many dog maladies, like canine hip dysplasia, which are not universally treated in the same manner. Some veterinarians opt for surgery more often than others do.

SELECTING A QUALIFIED VETERINARIAN

Your selection of a veterinarian should not be based solely upon personality (as most are) but also upon his convenience to your home. You want a vet who is close because you might have emergencies or need to make multiple visits for treatments. You want a vet who has services that you might require, such as a boarding kennel and grooming facilities, as well as sophisticated pet supplies and a good reputation for ability and responsiveness. There is nothing

Before you buy your Dalmatian, meet and interview the veterinarians in your area. Take everything into consideration—discuss their backgrounds, specialties, fees, emergency policies, etc.

more frustrating than having to wait a day or more to get a response from your veterinarian. You should also talk to your prospective choices to make sure that he or she has experience dealing with the Dalmatian's unique veterinary needs. Although most Dalmatians remain healthy throughout their lives, you want to rest assured that help will be available should the need arise.

All veterinarians are licensed and their diplomas and/or certificates should be displayed in their waiting rooms. There are, however, many veterinary specialties that usually require further studies and internships. There are specialists in heart problems (veterinary cardiologists), skin problems (veterinary dermatologists), teeth and gum problems (veterinary dentists), eye problems (veterinary ophthalmologists), x-rays (veterinary radiologists), and surgeons who have specialties in bones, muscles or other organs. Most veterinarians do

Breakdown of Veterinary Income by Category

%	Category
2%	Dentistry
4%	Radiology
12%	Surgery
15%	Vaccinations
19%	Laboratory
23%	Examinations
25%	Medicines

routine surgery such as neutering, stitching up wounds and docking tails for those breeds in which such is required for show purposes. When the problem affecting your dog is serious, it is not unusual or impudent to get another medical opinion. You might also want to compare costs among several veterinarians. Sophisticated health care and veterinary services can be very costly. Don't be bashful about discussing these costs with your veterinarian or his (her) staff. It is not infrequent that important decisions are based upon financial considerations.

A typical vet's income, categorized according to services performed. This survey dealt with small-animal (pets) practices.

PREVENTATIVE MEDICINE
It is much easier, less costly and more effective to practice preventative medicine than to fight bouts of illness and disease. Properly bred puppies come from parents that were selected based upon their

The Dalmatian's skin and coat can encounter some unique problems that may require the advice of a specialist.

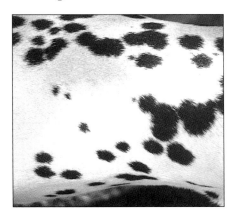

The first weeks of life spent nursing and bonding are crucial to a puppy's future health and behavior.

genetic disease profile. Both parents should have tested normal for bilateral hearing. The dam should have been vaccinated, free of all internal and external parasites and properly nourished. For these reasons, a visit to the veterinarian who cared for the dam (mother) is recommended. The dam can pass on disease resistance to her puppies, which can last for eight to ten weeks, but she can also pass on parasites and many infections. That's why you should visit the veterinarian who cared for the dam.

WEANING TO FIVE MONTHS OLD

Puppies should be weaned by the time they are about two months old. A puppy that remains for at least eight weeks with its mother and littermates usually adapts better to other dogs and people later in its life.

Some new owners have their puppy examined by a veterinarian immediately, which is a good idea. Vaccination programs usually begin

when the puppy is very young.

The puppy will have its teeth examined and have its skeletal conformation and general health checked prior to certification by the veterinarian. Puppies in certain breeds have problems with their kneecaps, eye cataracts and other eye problems, heart murmurs and undescended testicles. They may also have personality problems, and your veterinarian might have training in temperament evaluation.

VACCINATION SCHEDULING

Most vaccinations are given by injection and should only be done by a veterinarian. Both he and you should keep a record of the date of the injection, the identification of the vaccine and the amount given. Some vets give a first vaccination at eight weeks, but most dog breeders prefer the course not to commence until about ten weeks because of negating any antibodies passed on by the dam. The

NEUTERING/SPAYING

Male dogs are castrated. The operation removes both testicles and requires that the dog be anesthetized. Recovery takes about one week. Females are spayed; in this operation, the uterus (womb) and both of the ovaries are removed. This is major surgery, also carried out under general anesthesia, and it usually takes a bitch two weeks to recover.

First Aid at a Glance

Burns
Place the affected area under cool water; use ice if only a small area is burnt.

Bee stings/Insect bites
Apply ice to relieve swelling; antihistamine dosed properly.

Animal bites
Clean any bleeding area; apply pressure until bleeding subsides; go to the vet.

Spider bites
Use cold compress and a pressurized pack to inhibit venom's spreading.

Antifreeze poisoning
Induce vomiting with hydrogen peroxide. Seek *immediate* veterinary help!

Fish hooks
Removal best handled by vet; hook must be cut in order to remove.

Snake bites
Pack ice around bite; contact vet quickly; identify snake for proper antivenin.

Car accident
Move dog from roadway with blanket; seek veterinary aid.

Shock
Calm the dog; keep him warm; seek immediate veterinary help.

Nosebleed
Apply cold compress to the nose; apply pressure to any visible abrasion.

Bleeding
Apply pressure above the area; treat wound by applying a cotton pack.

Heat stroke
Submerge dog in cold bath; cool down with fresh air and water; go to the vet.

Frostbite/Hypothermia
Warm the dog with a warm bath, electric blankets or hot water bottles.

Abrasions
Clean the wound and wash out thoroughly with fresh water; apply antiseptic.

 Remember: an injured dog may attempt to bite a helping hand from fear and confusion. Always muzzle the dog before trying to offer assistance.

HEALTH AND VACCINATION SCHEDULE

AGE IN WEEKS:	6TH	8TH	10TH	12TH	14TH	16TH	20-24TH	52ND
Worm Control	✔	✔	✔	✔	✔	✔	✔	
Neutering							✔	
Heartworm		✔		✔		✔	✔	
Parvovirus	✔		✔		✔		✔	✔
Distemper		✔		✔		✔		✔
Hepatitis		✔		✔		✔		✔
Leptospirosis								✔
Parainfluenza	✔		✔		✔			✔
Dental Examination		✔					✔	✔
Complete Physical		✔					✔	✔
Coronavirus				✔			✔	✔
Canine Cough	✔							
Hip Dysplasia							✔	
Rabies							✔	

Vaccinations are not instantly effective. It takes about two weeks for the dog's immune system to develop antibodies. Most vaccinations require annual booster shots. Your vet should guide you in this regard.

vaccination scheduling is usually based on a 15-day cycle. You must take your vet's advice as to when to vaccinate as this may differ according to the vaccine used. Most vaccinations immunize your puppy against viruses.

The usual vaccines contain immunizing doses of several different viruses such as distemper, parvovirus, parain-fluenza and hepatitis. There are other vaccines available when the puppy is at risk. You should rely upon professional advice. This is especially true for the booster-shot program. Most vaccination programs require a booster when the puppy is a year old and once a year thereafter. In some cases,

VACCINE ALLERGIES

Vaccines do not work all the time. Sometimes dogs are allergic to them and many times the antibodies, which are supposed to be stimulated by the vaccine, just are not produced. You should keep your dog in the veterinary clinic for an hour after it is vaccinated to be sure there are no allergic reactions.

circumstances may require more frequent immunizations. Kennel cough, more formally known as tracheobronchitis, is treated with a vaccine that is sprayed into the dog's nostrils. Kennel cough is usually included in routine vaccination, but this is often not so effective as for other major diseases.

FIVE MONTHS TO ONE YEAR OF AGE
Unless you intend to breed or show your dog, neutering (for males) or spaying (for females) the puppy at six months of age is recommended. Discuss this with your veterinarian, as this procedure has proven to be extremely beneficial to both male and female puppies. Besides eliminating the possibility of pregnancy, it inhibits (but does not prevent) breast cancer in bitches and prostate cancer in male dogs. Under no circumstances should a bitch be spayed prior to her first season.

DOGS OLDER THAN ONE YEAR
Continue to visit the veterinarian at least once a year. There is no such

DISEASE REFERENCE CHART

	What is it?	What causes it?	Symptoms
Leptospirosis	Severe disease that affects the internal organs; can be spread to people.	A bacterium, which is often carried by rodents, that enters through mucous membranes and spreads quickly throughout the body.	Range from fever, vomiting and loss of appetite in less severe cases to shock, irreversible kidney damage and possibly death in most severe cases.
Rabies	Potentially deadly virus that infects warm-blooded mammals.	Bite from a carrier of the virus, mainly wild animals.	1st stage: dog exhibits change in behavior, fear. 2nd stage: dog's behavior becomes more aggressive. 3rd stage: loss of coordination, trouble with bodily functions.
Parvovirus	Highly contagious virus, potentially deadly.	Ingestion of the virus, which is usually spread through the feces of infected dogs.	Most common: severe diarrhea. Also vomiting, fatigue, lack of appetite.
Canine cough	Contagious respiratory infection.	Combination of types of bacteria and virus. Most common: *Bordetella bronchiseptica* bacteria and parainfluenza virus.	Chronic cough.
Distemper	Disease primarily affecting respiratory and nervous system.	Virus that is related to the human measles virus.	Mild symptoms such as fever, lack of appetite and mucus secretion progress to evidence of brain damage, "hard pad."
Hepatitis	Virus primarily affecting the liver.	Canine adenovirus type I (CAV-1). Enters system when dog breathes in particles.	Lesser symptoms include listlessness, diarrhea, vomiting. More severe symptoms include "blue-eye" (clumps of virus in eye).
Coronavirus	Virus resulting in digestive problems.	Virus is spread through infected dog's feces.	Stomach upset evidenced by lack of appetite, vomiting, diarrhea.

disease as old age, but bodily functions do change with age. The eyes and ears are no longer as efficient. Liver, kidney and intestinal functions often decline. Proper dietary changes, recommended by your veterinarian, can make life more pleasant for the aging Dalmatian and you.

SKIN PROBLEMS IN DALMATIANS

Veterinarians are consulted by dog owners for skin problems more than for any other group of diseases or maladies.

DENTAL HEALTH

A dental examination is in order when the dog is between six months and one year of age so that any permanent teeth that have erupted incorrectly can be corrected. It is important to begin a brushing routine at home, using dental-care products made for dogs, such as special toothbrushes and toothpaste. Durable nylon and safe edible chews should be a part of your puppy's arsenal for good health, good teeth and pleasant breath. The vast majority of dogs three to four years old and older has diseases of the gums from lack of dental attention. Using the various types of dental chews can be very effective in controlling dental plaque.

Dogs' skin is almost as sensitive as human skin and both suffer from almost the same ailments (though the occurrence of acne in dogs is rare!). For this reason, veterinary dermatology has developed into a specialty practiced by many veterinarians.

Since many skin problems have visual symptoms that are almost identical, it requires the skill of an experienced veterinary dermatologist to identify and cure many of the more severe skin disorders. Pet shops sell many treatments for skin problems, but most of the treatments are directed at symptoms and not the underlying problem(s). If your dog is suffering from a skin disorder, you should seek professional assistance as quickly as possible. As with all diseases, the earlier a problem is identified and treated, the more successful is the cure.

HEREDITARY SKIN DISORDERS

Veterinary dermatologists are currently researching a number of skin disorders that are believed to have a hereditary basis. These inherited diseases are transmitted by both parents, who appear (phenotypically) normal but have a recessive gene for the disease, meaning that they carry, but are not affected by, the disease. These diseases pose serious problems to breeders because in some instances there are no methods of identifying carriers. Often the secondary diseases associated with these skin conditions are even more debilitating than the skin disorders themselves, including cancers and respiratory problems; others can be lethal.

Among the hereditary skin disorders, for which the mode of inheritance is known, are: acrodermatitis, cutaneous asthenia (Ehlers-Danlos syndrome), sebaceous adenitis, cyclic hematopoiesis, dermatomyositis, IgA deficiency, color dilution alopecia and nodular dermatofibrosis. Some of these disorders are limited to one or two breeds, while others affect a large number of breeds. All inherited diseases must be diagnosed and treated by a veterinarian.

PARASITE BITES

Many of us are allergic to insect bites. The bites itch, erupt and may even become infected. Dogs have the same reaction to fleas, ticks and/or mites. When an insect lands on you, you have the chance to whisk it away with your hand. Unfortunately, when your dog is bitten by a flea, tick or mite, he can only scratch it away or bite it. By the time the dog has been bitten, the parasite has done some of its damage. It may also have laid eggs, which will cause further problems in the near future. The itching from parasite bites is probably due to the saliva injected into the site when the parasite sucks the dog's blood.

A SKUNKY PROBLEM

Have you noticed your dog dragging his rump along the floor? If so, it is likely that his anal sacs are impacted or possibly infected. The anal sacs are small pouches located on both sides of the anus under the skin and muscles. They are about the size and shape of a grape and contain a foul-smelling liquid. Their contents are usually emptied when the dog has a bowel movement but, if not emptied completely, they will impact, which will cause your dog much pain. Fortunately, your veterinarian can tend to this problem easily by draining the sacs for the dog. Be aware that your dog might also empty his anal sacs in cases of extreme fright.

AUTO-IMMUNE SKIN CONDITIONS

Auto-immune skin conditions are commonly referred to as being allergic to yourself, while allergies are usually inflammatory reactions to outside stimuli. Auto-immune diseases cause serious damage to the tissues.

The best known auto-immune disease is lupus, which affects people as well as dogs. The symptoms are variable and may affect the kidneys, bones, blood chemistry and skin. It can be fatal to both dogs and humans, though it is not thought to be transmissible. It is usually successfully treated with cortisone, prednisone or similar

HOW TO PREVENT BLOAT

Research has confirmed that the structure of deep-chested breeds contributes to their predisposition to bloat. Nevertheless, here are some precautions that you can take to reduce the risk of this condition:

- Feed your dog twice daily rather than offer one big meal.
- Do not exercise your dog for at least one hour before and two hours after he has eaten.
- Make certain that your dog is calm and not overly excited while he is eating. It has been proven that nervous or overly excited dogs are more prone to develop bloat.
- Add a small portion of moist meat product to his dry food ration.
- Serve his meals in an elevated bowl stand, which avoids the dog's craning his neck while eating.
- To prevent your dog from gobbling his food too quickly, and thereby swallowing air, put some large (unswallowable) toys into his bowl so that he will have to eat around them to get his food.
- Never allow him to gulp water.

corticosteroid, but extensive use of these drugs can have harmful side effects.

ACRAL LICK GRANULOMA

Dalmatians and other dogs about the same size (like Labrador Retrievers) have a very poorly understood syndrome called acral lick. The manifestation of the problem is the dog's tireless attack on a specific area of the body, almost always the front legs. The dog licks so intensively that he removes the hair and skin, leaving a large ugly wound. There is no absolute cure, but corticosteroids are the most common treatment.

PYODERMA

Referred to more colloquially as "Dalmatian crud," pyoderma is relatively common in the Dalmatian. Pyoderma is caused by *Staphylococcus intermedius,* a bacterium. While bacteria naturally exist on dogs' skin without causing a problem, factors such as stress or contact irritants can cause the bacteria to infect the skin. Pyoderma is normally treated with antibiotics and medicated shampoos. If an underlying cause, such as an allergy, can be determined, then this should be treated as well. Recurrent pyoderma for which an underlying cause cannot be determined requires the help of a veterinary dermatologist. This condition does not cause the dog pain or itching; it mainly affects the coat's appearance.

DALMATIAN BRONZING SYNDROME

It is now generally known that there is no singular disorder, or "syndrome," that causes bronzing in the Dalmatian. "Bronzing," which is a term for black hair that has turned brown on the ends, is also used in conjunction with skin problems to indicate discoloration of the skin and coat. Because of the Dal's white coat, skin problems usually manifest themselves as brown, unhealthy-looking patches. Dalmatians with abnormalities of the skin and coat need individual treatment and have individual problems; there is no particular panacea for all problems that result in a "bronze" appearance.

AIRBORNE ALLERGIES

An interesting allergy is pollen allergy. Humans have hay fever, rose fever and other fevers from

SIMULATED MEDICAL CONDITION FOR EDUCATIONAL PURPOSES ONLY

Acral lick granuloma results in an ugly wound, usually on the leg. No one knows why a dog starts attacking a single spot so intensively. Vets can treat the problem.

which they suffer during the pollinating season. Many dogs suffer from the same types of inhalant allergies, which are extremely common in the Dalmatian. When the pollen count is high, your dog might suffer, but don't expect him to sneeze and have a runny nose like humans. Dogs react to pollen allergies the same way they react to fleas—they scratch and bite themselves.

Dogs, like humans, can be

tested for allergens. Discuss the testing with your veterinary dermatologist.

FOOD PROBLEMS

FOOD ALLERGIES

Dogs are allergic to many foods that are best-sellers and highly recommended by breeders and veterinarians. Changing the brand of food that you buy may not eliminate the problem if the element to which the dog is allergic is contained in the new brand.

Your dog can be releasing a huge quantity of worm eggs every time he defecates. Sometimes these eggs can live in the grass and infect humans. The dog's relief area should be in a remote area of the yard, and always clean up the droppings.

THE SAME ALLERGIES

Chances are that you and your dog will have the same allergies. Your allergies are readily recognizable and usually easily treated. Your dog's allergies may be masked.

Recognizing a food allergy is difficult. Humans vomit or have rashes when they eat a food to which they are allergic. Dogs neither vomit nor (usually) develop a rash. They react in the same manner as they do to an airborne or flea allergy: they itch, scratch and bite, thus making the diagnosis extremely difficult. While pollen allergies and parasite bites are usually seasonal, food allergies are year-round problems.

FOOD INTOLERANCE

Food intolerance is the inability of the dog to completely digest certain foods. For example, puppies that may have done very well on their mother's milk may not do well on cows' milk. The result of this food intolerance may be loose bowels, passing gas and stomach pains. These are the only obvious symptoms of food intolerance and that makes diagnosis difficult.

TREATING FOOD PROBLEMS

It is possible to handle food allergies and food intolerance yourself. Put your Dalmatian on a diet that it has never had. Obviously if it has never eaten this new food it can't have been allergic or intolerant of it. You should already be consulting with your vet about what you feed your Dalmatian, so ask him for advice on how to safely switch what you are feeding. Start with a single ingredient that is not in the dog's diet at the present time. Many ingredients are common in commercial dog foods, so try something less commonly used, being careful to stay away from high-protein, especially high-purine, foods for your Dalmatian. Keep the dog on this diet (with no additives) for a month. If the symptoms of food allergy or intolerance disappear, chances are your dog has a food allergy.

Don't think that the single ingredient cured the problem. You still must find a suitable diet and ascertain which ingredient in the old diet was objectionable. This is most easily done by adding ingredients to the new diet one at a time. Let the dog stay on the modified diet for a month before you add another ingredient. Eventually, you will determine the ingredient that caused the adverse reaction.

HEALTH PROBLEMS FREQUENTLY SEEN IN THE DALMATIAN

DEAFNESS

One of the problems most commonly associated with the Dalmatian is deafness. While studies have shown that less than 10 percent, which is still a high percentage in a single breed, of Dalmatians are completely deaf, close to 25 percent of the breed is born deaf in one ear. Thus, BAER (Brainstem Auditory Evoked Response) testing is extremely important for the Dalmatian and other breeds with high deafness rates (e.g., Bull Terrier). A simple explanation of this test is that it is a painless procedure in which sounds are administered to the

dog, and then the sound waves are analyzed to see if they are picked up by the dogs' ears and transmitted to the brain. Small electrodes inserted under the dog's skin analyze the sound waves' transmission from the ear drum to the cochlea and eventually to the brain. The Dalmatian Club of America recommends that *all* litters be BAER tested.

In order to eliminate deafness from the breed, dogs that exhibit deafness in one or both ears should never be bred. BAER testing is the only reliable way to determine a Dalmatian's hearing; do not buy a puppy who has not been tested. Deaf pups and dogs can often adapt to the point that their reactions and behavior appear normal to the human eye. Don't take a breeder's word that his dogs can hear; only buy a pup from a BAER-tested litter that comes from BAER-tested normal parents.

URINARY INFECTION AND STONE FORMING

Stone-forming has become a major problem in the Dalmatian and certain other breeds. Certain sources of protein yield high amounts of purines, which are known to cause urinary stones in Dalmatians. Purine-rich foods include meat and related by-products, and these foods should not be fed to the Dalmatian in favor of alternative protein

Dalmatian puppies will investigate anything they find that is chewable. Always provide safe chew toys and make sure that anything dangerous is kept out of reach, both inside the home and in the yard.

sources such as lamb and turkey in a rice-, vegetable- or barley-based dog food. Another essential preventative is plenty of water. For dogs that are proven stone-formers, distilled water may be necessary.

Routine urine testing is necessary for stone-formers. These tests are relatively simple, requiring the owner to collect a pre-feeding urine sample from the Dalmatian and determine the urine's acidity with a litmus-paper-type dipstick, which is available from the veterinarian. Acidic urine promotes the growth of urinary crystals, and testing helps the owner determine when to modify treatment to lessen the acidity.

HYPOTHYROIDISM

Hypothyroidism is one of the most common endocrine problems in dogs in general, and the most common endocrine problem in Dalmatians. This is a condition in which the dog does not produce enough thyroid hormones. Although people often associate obesity with hypothyroidism as the most common symptom, this is not the case. Some dogs may appear obese, even if eating less, but symptoms such as lethargy and recurrent infection are more indicative of hypothyroidism. Laboratory tests are the only way to definitely diagnose the condition.

Treatment, which is extremely successful, consists of daily supplementation with thyroid hormones.

IGA DEFICIENCY

IgA deficiency is relatively common in humans and has been found in dogs, including the Dalmatian, as well. IgA is a protein; it is a part of the immune system that protects the epithelial surfaces of the mucous membranes in the respiratory and digestive systems against foreign

PET ADVANTAGES

If you do not intend to show or breed your new puppy, your veterinarian will probably recommend that you spay your female or neuter your male. Some people believe neutering leads to weight gain, but if you feed and exercise your dog properly, this is easily avoided. Spaying or neutering can actually have many positive outcomes, such as:

- training becomes easier, as the dog focuses less on the urge to mate and more on you!
- females are protected from unplanned pregnancy as well as ovarian and uterine cancers.
- males are guarded from testicular tumors and have a reduced risk of developing prostate cancer.

Talk to your vet regarding the right age to spay/neuter and other aspects of the procedure.

particles. Without IgA, these sufaces are more vulnerable to "attack" by bacteria, viruses, etc., and thus the body's systems become more open to disease. Pups receive IgA in their mother's milk, but in affected dogs IgA quantities do not grow to sufficient levels. There is no cure for the disorder but the symptoms, which are commonly various types of skin problems, can be treated to keep the dog comfortable. This is a hereditary condition, so obviously affected dogs should never be bred from.

BLOAT (GASTRIC DILATATION)

Bloat, also known as gastric dilatation/volvulus or gastric torsion, is common in the Dalmatian. This condition is caused by too much air in the stomach, either from swallowing air or from air produced by the digestive system. When the stomach is full of air, it can twist on itself, thus cutting off the flow of food and blood. As the stomach becomes more bloated and the tissues are without blood for lengthening periods of time, shock will occur and, eventually, death.

The Dalmatian is prone to bloat for several reasons: first, because larger deep-chested breeds are more susceptible; second, because Dals have both a love of food, and therefore a tendency to gulp, and a love of running around, two things which

> **BE CAREFUL WHERE YOU WALK YOUR DOG**
> Dogs who have been exposed to lawns sprayed with herbicides have double and triple the rate of malignant lymphoma. Suburban dogs are especially at risk, as they are exposed to manicured lawns and gardens. Dogs perspire and absorb through their footpads. Be careful where your dog walks and always avoid any area that appears yellowed from chemical overspray. These chemicals are not good for you, either!

increase the probability of introducing air into the stomach.

If the dog looks restless or uncomfortable, or has a visibly distended abdomen, treatment is needed right away, as the dog could go into shock in just a few hours. Surgery may be necessary.

Feeding several small meals throughout the day rather than one large one and elevating the dog's bowls so that he does not have to crane his neck to reach them are two preventative measures. Also, do not allow the dog free exercise for at least 2 hours before and after mealtime, and try to prevent him from gulping food and water. While water should be available to the Dalmatian throughout the day, he should be offered only a minimal amount directly following a meal.

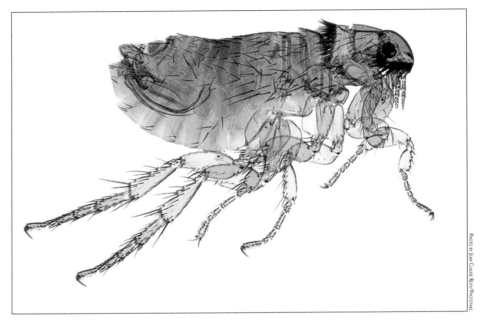

A male dog flea, *Ctenocephalides canis.*

PHOTO BY JEAN CLAUDE REVY/PHOTOTAKE

EXTERNAL PARASITES

FLEAS

Of all the problems to which dogs are prone, none is more well known and frustrating than fleas. Flea infestation is relatively simple to cure but difficult to prevent. Parasites that are harbored inside the body are a bit more difficult to eradicate but they are easier to control.

To control flea infestation, you have to understand the flea's life cycle. Fleas are often thought of as a summertime problem, but centrally heated homes have changed the patterns and fleas can be found at any time of the year. The most effective method of flea control is a two-stage approach: one stage to kill the adult fleas, and the other to control the development of pre-adult fleas. Unfortunately, no single active ingredient is effective against all stages of the life cycle.

FLEA KILLER CAUTION— "POISON"

Flea-killers are poisonous. You should not spray these toxic chemicals on areas of a dog's body that he licks, including his genitals and his face. Flea killers taken internally are a better answer, but check with your vet in case internal therapy is not advised for your dog.

LIFE CYCLE STAGES

During its life, a flea will pass through four life stages: egg, larva, pupa or nymph and adult. The adult stage is the most visible and irritating stage of the flea life cycle, and this is why the majority of flea-control products concentrate on this stage. The fact is that adult fleas account for only 1% of the total flea population, and the other 99% exist in pre-adult stages, i.e., eggs, larvae and nymphs. The pre-adult stages are barely visible to the naked eye.

THE LIFE CYCLE OF THE FLEA

Eggs are laid on the dog, usually in quantities of about 20 or 30, several times a day. The adult female flea must have a blood meal before each egg-laying session. When first laid, the eggs will cling to the dog's hair, as the eggs are still moist. However, they will quickly dry out and fall from the dog, especially if the dog moves around or scratches. Many eggs will fall off in the dog's favorite area or an area in which he spends a lot of time, such as his bed.

Once the eggs fall from the dog onto the carpet or furniture, they will hatch into larvae. This takes from one to ten days. Larvae are not particularly mobile and will usually travel only a few inches from where they hatch. However, they do have a tendency to move away from bright light and heavy

> **EN GARDE:**
> **CATCHING FLEAS OFF GUARD!**
> Consider the following ways to arm yourself against fleas:
> - Add a small amount of pennyroyal or eucalyptus oil to your dog's bath. These natural remedies repel fleas.
> - Supplement your dog's food with fresh garlic (minced or grated) and a hearty amount of brewer's yeast, both of which ward off fleas.
> - Use a flea comb on your dog daily. Submerge fleas in a cup of bleach to kill them quickly.
> - Confine the dog to only a few rooms to limit the spread of fleas in the home.
> - Vacuum daily...and get all of the crevices! Dispose of the bag every few days until the problem is under control.
> - Wash your dog's bedding daily. Cover cushions where your dog sleeps with towels, and wash the towels often.

traffic—under furniture and behind doors are common places to find high quantities of flea larvae.

The flea larvae feed on dead organic matter, including adult flea feces, until they are ready to change into adult fleas. Fleas will usually remain as larvae for around seven days. After this period, the larvae will pupate into protective pupae. While inside the pupae, the larvae will undergo metamorphosis and change into adult fleas. This can take as little time as a few days, but the adult fleas can remain inside the pupae waiting to hatch for up to two years. The pupae are signaled to hatch by certain stimuli, such as physical pressure—the pupae's being stepped on, heat from an animal's lying on the pupae or increased carbon-dioxide levels and vibrations—indicating that a suitable host is available.

Once hatched, the adult flea must feed within a few days. Once the adult flea finds a host, it will not leave voluntarily. It only becomes dislodged by grooming or the host animal's scratching. The adult flea will remain on the

host for the duration of its life unless forcibly removed.

TREATING THE ENVIRONMENT AND THE DOG

Treating fleas should be a two-pronged attack. First, the environment needs to be treated; this includes carpets and furniture, especially the dog's bedding and areas underneath furniture. The environment should be treated with a household spray containing an Insect Growth Regulator (IGR) and an insecticide to kill the adult fleas. Most IGRs are effective against eggs and larvae; they actually mimic the fleas' own hormones and stop the eggs and larvae from developing into adult fleas. There are currently no treatments available to attack the pupa stage of the life cycle, so the adult insecticide is used to kill the newly hatched adult fleas before they find a host. Most IGRs are active for many months, while adult insecticides are only active

A scanning electron micrograph of a dog or cat flea, *Ctenocephalides*, magnified more than 100x. This image has been colorized for effect.

THE LIFE CYCLE OF THE FLEA

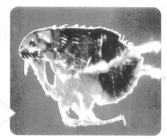

Adult

**Pupa
or
Nymph**

Egg

Larva

Fleas have been around for millions of years and have adapted to changing host animals. They are able to go through a complete life cycle in less than one month or they can extend their lives to almost two years by remaining as pupae or cocoons. They do not need blood or any other food for up to 20 months.

INSECT GROWTH REGULATOR (IGR)

Two types of products should be used when treating fleas—a product to treat the pet and a product to treat the home. Adult fleas represent less than 1% of the flea population. The pre-adult fleas (eggs, larvae and pupae) represent more than 99% of the flea population and are found in the environment; it is in the case of pre-adult fleas that products containing an Insect Growth Regulator (IGR) should be used in the home.

IGRs are a new class of compounds used to prevent the development of insects. They do not kill the insect outright, but instead use the insect's biology against it to stop it from completing its growth. Products that contain methoprene are the world's first and leading IGRs. Used to control fleas and other insects, this type of IGR will stop flea larvae from developing and protect the house for up to seven months.

The American dog tick, *Dermacentor variabilis*, is probably the most common tick found on dogs. Look at the strength in its eight legs! No wonder it's hard to detach them.

for a few days.

When treating with a household spray, it is a good idea to vacuum before applying the product. This stimulates as many pupae as possible to hatch into adult fleas. The vacuum cleaner should also be treated with an insecticide to prevent the eggs and larvae that have been collected in the vacuum bag from hatching.

The second stage of treatment is to apply an adult insecticide to the dog. Traditionally, this would be in the form of a collar or a spray, but more recent innovations include digestible insecticides that poison the fleas when they ingest the dog's blood. Alternatively, there are drops that, when placed on the back of the dog's neck, spread throughout the hair and skin to kill adult fleas.

TICKS

Though not as common as fleas, ticks are found all over the tropical and temperate world. They don't bite, like fleas; they harpoon. They dig their sharp proboscis (nose) into the dog's skin and drink the blood. Their only food and drink is dog's

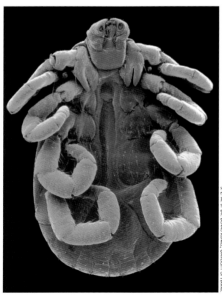

S. E. M. BY DR. DENNIS KUNKEL, UNIVERSITY OF HAWAII

blood. Dogs can get Lyme disease, Rocky Mountain spotted fever, tick bite paralysis and many other diseases from ticks. They may live where fleas are found and they like to hide in cracks or seams in walls. They are controlled the same way fleas are controlled.

The American dog tick, *Dermacentor variabilis*, may well be the most common dog tick in many geographical areas, especially those areas where the climate is hot and humid. Most dog ticks have life expectancies of a week to six months, depending upon climatic conditions. They can neither jump nor fly, but they can crawl slowly and can range up to 16 feet to reach a sleeping or unsuspecting dog.

MITES

Just as fleas and ticks can be problematic for your dog, mites can also lead to an itchy nuisance. Microscopic in size, mites are related to ticks and generally take up permanent residence on their host animal— in this case, your dog! The term *mange* refers to any infestation caused by one of the mighty mites, of which there are six varieties that concern dog owners.

Demodex mites cause a condition known as demodicosis (sometimes called red mange or

DEER-TICK CROSSING

The great outdoors may be fun for your dog, but it also is a home to dangerous ticks. Deer ticks carry a bacterium known as *Borrelia burgdorferi* and are most active in the autumn and spring. When infections are caught early, penicillin and tetracycline are effective antibiotics, but, if left untreated, the bacteria may cause neurological, kidney and cardiac problems as well as long-term trouble with walking and painful joints.

S. E. M. BY DR. ANDREW SPIELMAN/PHOTOTAKE.

PHOTO BY DR. DENNIS KUNKEL, UNIVERSITY OF HAWAII.

The head of an American dog tick, *Dermacentor variabilis*, enlarged and colorized for effect.

follicular mange), in which the mites live in the dog's hair follicles and sebaceous glands in larger-than-normal numbers. This type of mange is commonly passed from the dam to her puppies and usually shows up on the puppies' muzzles, though demodicosis is not transferable from one normal dog to another. Most dogs recover from this type of mange without any treatment, though topical therapies are commonly prescribed by the vet.

The *Cheyletiellosis* mite is the hook-mouthed culprit associated with "walking dandruff," a condition that affects dogs as well as cats and rabbits. This mite lives on the surface of the animal's skin and is readily transferable through direct or indirect contact with an affected animal. The dandruff is present in the form of scaly skin, which may or may not be itchy. If not treated, this mange can affect a whole kennel of dogs and can be spread to humans as well.

The *Sarcoptes* mite causes intense itching on the dog in the form of a condition known as scabies or sarcoptic mange. The cycle of the *Sarcoptes* mite lasts about three weeks, and the mites live in the top layer of the dog's skin (epidermis), preferably in areas with little hair. Scabies is highly contagious and can be passed to humans. Sometimes an allergic reaction to the mite worsens the severe itching associated with sarcoptic mange.

Ear mites, *Otodectes cynotis,* lead to otodectic mange, which most commonly affects the outer ear canal of the dog, though other areas can be affected as well. Dogs with ear-mite infestation commonly scratch at their ears, causing further irritation, and shake their heads. Dark brown droppings in the outer ear confirm the diagnosis. Your vet can prescribe a treatment to flush out the ears and kill any eggs in the ears. A complete month of treatment is necessary to cure the mange.

Two other mites, less common in dogs, include *Dermanyssus gallinae* (the poultry or red mite) and *Eutrombicula alfreddugesi* (the North American mite associated with trombiculidiasis or chigger infestation). The poultry mite frequently lives on chickens, but can transfer to dogs who spend time near farm animals. Chigger infestation affects dogs in the

DO NOT MIX
Never mix parasite-control products without first consulting your vet. Some products can become toxic when combined with others and can cause fatal consequences.

NOT A DROP TO DRINK
Never allow your dog to swim in polluted water or public areas where water quality can be suspect. Even perfectly clear water can harbor parasites, many of which can cause serious to fatal illnesses in canines. Areas inhabited by waterfowl and other wildlife are especially dangerous.

Central US who have exposure to woodlands. The types of mange caused by both of these mites are treatable by vets.

INTERNAL PARASITES
Most animals—fishes, birds and mammals, including dogs and humans—have worms and other parasites that live inside their bodies. According to Dr. Herbert R. Axelrod, the fish pathologist, there are two kinds of parasites: dumb and smart. The smart parasites live in peaceful cooperation with their hosts (symbiosis), while the dumb parasites kill their hosts. Most worm infections are relatively easy to control. If they are not controlled, they weaken the host dog to the point that other medical problems occur, but they do not kill the host as dumb parasites would.

A brown dog tick, *Rhipicephalus sanguineus*, is an uncommon but annoying tick found on dogs. Photo by Carolina Biological Supply/Phototake.

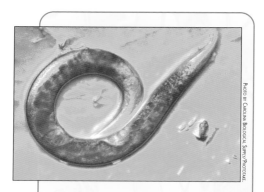

PHOTO BY CAROLINA BIOLOGICAL SUPPLY/PHOTOTAKE

The roundworm *Rhabditis* can infect both dogs and humans.

ROUNDWORMS

Average-size dogs can pass 1,360,000 roundworm eggs every day. For example, if there were only 1 million dogs in the world, the world would be saturated with thousands of tons of dog feces. These feces would contain around 15,000,000,000 roundworm eggs.

Up to 31% of home yards and children's sand boxes in the US contain roundworm eggs.

Flushing dog's feces down the toilet is not a safe practice because the usual sewage treatments do not destroy roundworm eggs.

Infected puppies start shedding roundworm eggs at three weeks of age. They can be infected by their mother's milk.

The roundworm, *Ascaris lumbricoides.*

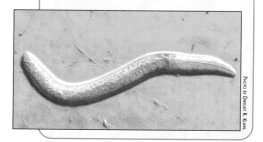

PHOTO BY DWIGHT R. KUHN

ROUNDWORMS

The roundworms that infect dogs are known scientifically as *Toxocara canis.* They live in the dog's intestines and shed eggs continually. It has been estimated that a dog produces about 6 or more ounces of feces every day. Each ounce of feces averages hundreds of thousands of roundworm eggs. There are no known areas in which dogs roam that do not contain roundworm eggs. The greatest danger of roundworms is that they infect people, too! It is wise to have your dog tested regularly for roundworms.

In young puppies, roundworms cause bloated bellies, diarrhea, coughing and vomiting, and are transmitted from the dam (through blood or milk). Affected puppies will not appear as animated as normal puppies. The worms appear spaghetti-like, measuring as long as 6 inches. Adult dogs can acquire roundworms through coprophagia (eating contaminated feces) or by killing rodents that carry roundworms.

Roundworm infection can kill puppies and cause severe problems in adults, as the hatched larvae travel to the lungs and trachea through the bloodstream. Cleanliness is the best preventative for roundworms. Always pick up after your dog and dispose of feces in appropriate receptacles.

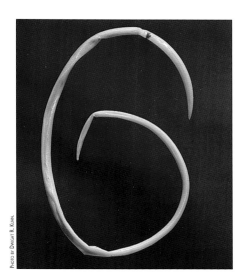

PHOTO BY DWIGHT R. KUHN

HOOKWORMS

In the United States, dog owners have to be concerned about four different species of hookworm, the most common and most serious of which is *Ancylostoma caninum,* which prefers warm climates. The others are *Ancylostoma braziliense, Ancylostoma tubaeforme* and *Uncinaria stenocephala,* the latter of which is a concern to dogs living in the Northern US and Canada, as this species prefers cold climates. Hookworms are dangerous to humans as well as to dogs and cats, and can be the cause of severe anemia due to iron deficiency. The worm uses its teeth to attach itself to the dog's intestines and changes the site of its attachment about six times per day. Each time the worm repositions itself, the dog loses blood and can become anemic. *Ancylostoma caninum* is the most likely of the four species to cause anemia in the dog.

Symptoms of hookworm infection include dark stools, weight loss, general weakness, pale coloration and anemia, as well as possible skin problems. Fortunately, hookworms are easily purged from the affected dog with a number of medications that have proven effective. Discuss these with your vet. Most heartworm preventatives include a hookworm insecticide as well.

Owners also must be aware that hookworms can infect humans, who can acquire the larvae through exposure to contaminated feces. Since the worms cannot complete their life cycle on a human, the worms simply infest the skin and cause irritation. This condition is known as cutaneous larva migrans syndrome. As a preventative, use disposable gloves or a "poop-scoop" to pick up your dog's droppings and prevent your dog (or neighborhood cats) from defecating in children's play areas.

The hookworm, *Ancylostoma caninum.*

PHOTO BY C. JAMES WEBB/PHOTOTAKE.

The infective stage of the hookworm larva.

TAPEWORMS

Humans, rats, squirrels, foxes, coyotes, wolves and domestic dogs are all susceptible to tapeworm infection. Except in humans, tapeworms are usually not a fatal infection. Infected individuals can harbor 1000 parasitic worms.

Tapeworms, like some other types of worm, are hermaphroditic, meaning male and female in the same worm.

If dogs eat infected rats or mice, or anything else infected with tapeworm, they get the tapeworm disease. One month after attaching to a dog's intestine, the worm starts shedding eggs. These eggs are infective immediately. Infective eggs can live for a few months without a host animal.

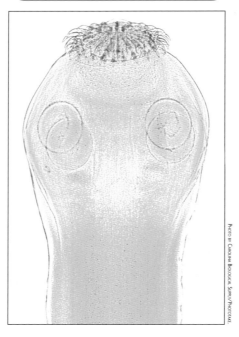

The head and rostellum (the round prominence on the scolex) of a tapeworm, which infects dogs and humans.

TAPEWORMS

There are many species of tapeworm, all of which are carried by fleas! The most common tapeworm affecting dogs is known as *Dipylidium caninum*. The dog eats the flea and starts the tapeworm cycle. Humans can also be infected with tapeworms—so don't eat fleas! Fleas are so small that your dog could pass them onto your hands, your plate or your food and thus make it possible for you to ingest a flea that is carrying tapeworm eggs.

While tapeworm infection is not life-threatening in dogs (smart parasite!), it can be the cause of a very serious liver disease for humans. About 50% of the humans infected with *Echinococcus multilocularis*, a type of tapeworm that causes alveolar hydatid, perish.

WHIPWORMS

In North America, whipworms are counted among the most common parasitic worms in dogs. The whipworm's scientific name is *Trichuris vulpis*. These worms attach themselves in the lower parts of the intestine, where they feed. Affected dogs may only experience upset tummies, colic and diarrhea. These worms, however, can live for months or years in the dog, beginning their larval stage in the small intestine, spending their adult stage in the large intestine and finally passing infective eggs through the dog's feces. The only way to detect whipworms is through a fecal examination, though this is not always foolproof. Treatment for whipworms is tricky, due to the worms' unusual life-cycle pattern, and very often dogs are reinfected due to exposure to infective eggs on the ground. The whipworm eggs can survive in the environment for as long as five years; thus, cleaning up droppings in your own backyard as well as in public places is absolutely essential for sanitation purposes and the health of your dog and others.

THREADWORMS
Though less common than roundworms, hookworms and those previously mentioned, threadworms concern dog owners in the Southwestern US and Gulf Coast area where the climate is hot and humid. Living in the small intestine of the dog, this worm measures a mere 2 millimeters and is round in shape. Like that of the whipworm, the threadworm's life cycle is very complex and the eggs and larvae are passed through the feces. A deadly disease in humans, *Strongyloides* readily infects people, and the handling of feces is the most common means of transmission. Threadworms are most often seen in young puppies; bloody diarrhea and pneumonia are symptoms. Sick puppies must be isolated and treated immediately; vets recommend a follow-up treatment one month later.

HEARTWORM PREVENTATIVES

There are many heartworm preventatives on the market, many of which are sold at your veterinarian's office. These products can be given daily or monthly, depending on the manufacturer's instructions. All of these preventatives contain chemical insecticides directed at killing heartworms, which leads to some controversy among dog owners. In effect, heartworm preventatives are necessary evils, though you should determine how necessary based on your pet's lifestyle. There is no doubt that heartworm is a dreadful disease that threatens the lives of dogs. However, the likelihood of your dog's being bitten by an infected mosquito is slim in most places, and a mosquito-repellent (or an herbal remedy such as Wormwood or Black Walnut) is much safer for your dog and will not compromise his immune system (the way heartworm preventatives will). Should you decide to use the traditional preventative "medications," you can consider giving the pill every other or third month. Since the toxins in the pill will kill the heartworms at all stages of development, the pill would be effective in killing larvae, nymphs or adults, and it takes four months for the larvae to reach the adult stage. Thus, there is no rationale to poisoning the dog's system on a monthly basis. Lastly, do not give the pill during the winter months since there are no mosquitoes around to pass on their infection, unless you live in a tropical environment.

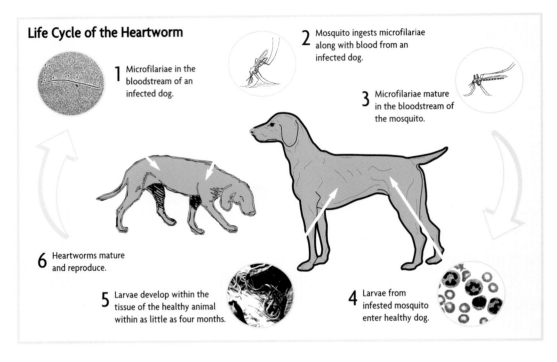

Life Cycle of the Heartworm

1 Microfilariae in the bloodstream of an infected dog.

2 Mosquito ingests microfilariae along with blood from an infected dog.

3 Microfilariae mature in the bloodstream of the mosquito.

4 Larvae from infested mosquito enter healthy dog.

5 Larvae develop within the tissue of the healthy animal within as little as four months.

6 Heartworms mature and reproduce.

HEARTWORMS

Heartworms are thin, extended worms up to 12 inches long, which live in a dog's heart and the major blood vessels surrounding it. Dogs may have up to 200 worms. Symptoms may be loss of energy, loss of appetite, coughing, the development of a pot belly and anemia.

Heartworms are transmitted by mosquitoes. The mosquito drinks the blood of an infected dog and takes in larvae with the blood. The larvae, called microfilariae, develop within the body of the mosquito and are passed on to the next dog bitten after the larvae mature. It takes two to three weeks for the larvae to develop to the infective stage within the body of the mosquito. Dogs are usually treated at about six weeks of age and maintained on a prophylactic dose given monthly.

Blood testing for heartworms is not necessarily indicative of how seriously your dog is infected. Although this is a dangerous disease, it is not easy for a dog to be infected. Discuss the various preventatives with your vet, as there are many different types now available. Together you can decide on a safe course of prevention for your dog.

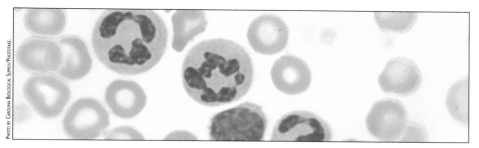

Magnified heartworm larvae, *Dirofilaria immitis.*

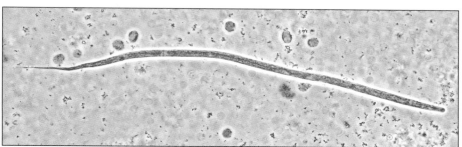

Heartworm, *Dirofilaria immitis.*

The heart of a dog infected with canine heartworm, *Dirofilaria immitis.*

Number-One Killer Disease in Dogs: CANCER

In every age, there is a word associated with a disease or plague that causes humans to shudder. In the 21st century, that word is "cancer." Just as cancer is the leading cause of death in humans, it claims nearly half the lives of dogs that die from a natural disease as well as half the dogs that die over the age of ten years.

Described as a genetic disease, cancer becomes a greater risk as the dog ages. Vets and dog owners have become increasingly aware of the threat of cancer to dogs. Statistics reveal that one dog in every five will develop cancer, the most common of which is skin cancer. Many cancers, including prostate, ovarian and breast cancer, can be avoided by spaying and neutering our dogs by the age of six months.

Early detection of cancer can save or extend a dog's life, so it is absolutely vital for owners to have their dogs examined by a qualified vet or oncologist immediately upon detection of any abnormality. Certain dietary guidelines have also proven to reduce the onset and spread of cancer. Foods based on fish rather than beef, due to the presence of Omega-3 fatty acids, are recommended. Other amino acids such as glutamine have significant benefits for canines, particularly those breeds that show a greater susceptibility to cancer.

Cancer management and treatments promise hope for future generations of canines. Since the disease is genetic, breeders should never breed a dog whose parents, grandparents and any related siblings have developed cancer. It is difficult to know whether to exclude an otherwise healthy dog from a breeding program, as the disease does not manifest itself until the dog's senior years.

RECOGNIZE CANCER WARNING SIGNS

Since early detection can possibly rescue your dog from becoming a cancer statistic, it is essential for owners to recognize the possible signs and seek the assistance of a qualified professional.

- Abnormal bumps or lumps that continue to grow
- Bleeding or discharge from any body cavity
- Persistent stiffness or lameness
- Recurrent sores or sores that do not heal
- Inappetence
- Breathing difficulties
- Weight loss
- Bad breath or odors
- General malaise and fatigue
- Eating and swallowing problems
- Difficulty urinating and defecating

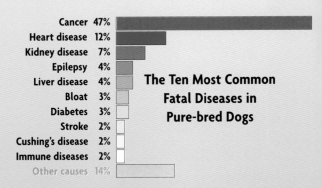

Cancer	47%
Heart disease	12%
Kidney disease	7%
Epilepsy	4%
Liver disease	4%
Bloat	3%
Diabetes	3%
Stroke	2%
Cushing's disease	2%
Immune diseases	2%
Other causes	14%

The Ten Most Common Fatal Diseases in Pure-bred Dogs

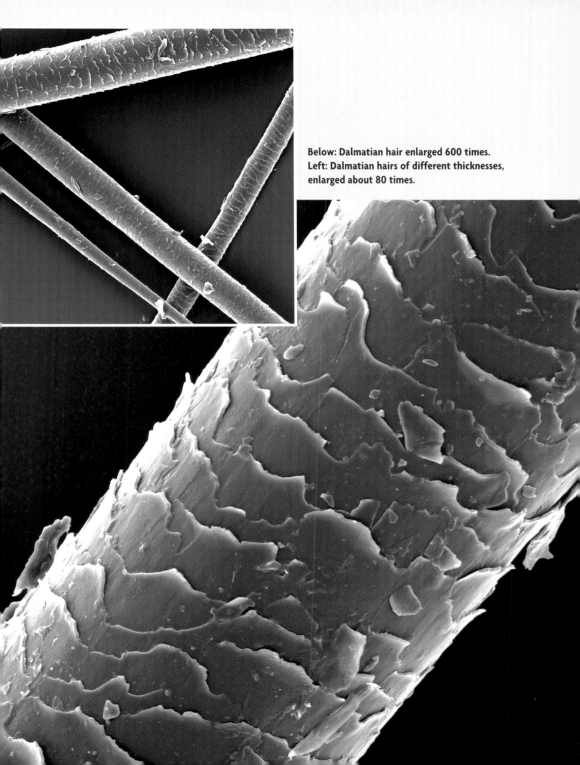

Below: Dalmatian hair enlarged 600 times.
Left: Dalmatian hairs of different thicknesses, enlarged about 80 times.

DO YOU KNOW ABOUT HIP DYSPLASIA?

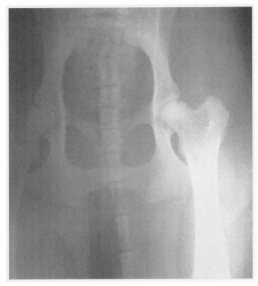

X-ray of a dog with "Good" hips.

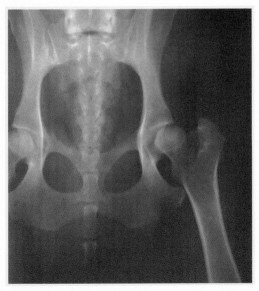

X-ray of a dog with "Moderate" dysplastic hips.

Hip dysplasia is a fairly common condition found in pure-bred dogs. When a dog has hip dysplasia, his hind leg has an incorrectly formed hip joint. By constant use of the hip joint, it becomes more and more loose, wears abnormally and may become arthritic.

Hip dysplasia can only be confirmed with an x-ray, but certain symptoms may indicate a problem. Your dog may have a hip dysplasia problem if he walks in a peculiar manner, hops instead of smoothly runs, uses his hind legs in unison (to keep the pressure off the weak joint), has trouble getting up from a prone position or always sits with both legs together on one side of his body.

As the dog matures, he may adapt well to life with a bad hip, but in a few years the arthritis develops and many dogs with hip dysplasia become crippled.

Hip dysplasia is considered an inherited disease and only can be diagnosed definitively by x-ray when the dog is two years old, although symptoms often appear earlier. Some experts claim that a special diet might help your puppy outgrow the bad hip, but the usual treatments are surgical. The removal of the pectineus muscle, the removal of the round part of the femur, reconstructing the pelvis and replacing the hip with an artificial one are all surgical interventions that are expensive, but they are usually very successful. Follow the advice of your veterinarian.

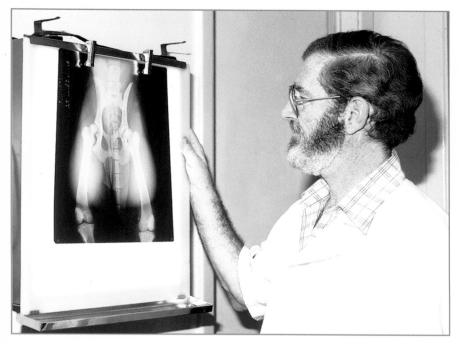

Left: A veterinarian evaluating a dog's x-ray for hip dysplasia. Diagnosis can only be made using radiographic techniques, which are interpreted (read) by a suitably trained veterinarian. Below: Illustrations of a three-year-old dog's elbow, manifesting elbow dysplasia with associated problems (acute, severe weight-bearing lameness of the right forelimb).

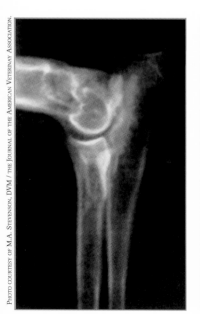
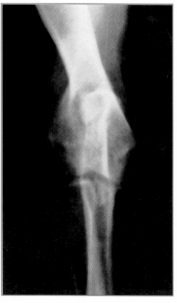
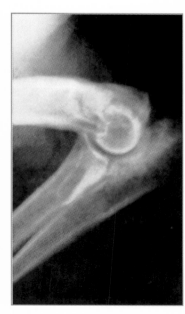

HOMEOPATHY:
an alternative
to conventional
medicine

"Less is Most"

Using this principle, the strength of a homeopathic remedy is measured by the number of serial dilutions that were undertaken to create it. The greater the number of serial dilutions, the greater the strength of the homeopathic remedy. The potency of a remedy that has been made by making a dilution of 1 part in 100 parts (or 1/100) is 1c or 1cH. If this remedy is subjected to a series of further dilutions, each one being 1/100, a more dilute and stronger remedy is produced. If the remedy is diluted in this way six times, it is called 6c or 6cH. A dilution of 6c is 1 part in 1,000,000,000,000. In general, higher potencies in more frequent doses are better for acute symptoms and lower potencies in more infrequent doses are more useful for chronic, long-standing problems.

CURING OUR DOGS NATURALLY

Holistic medicine means treating the whole animal as a unique, perfect, living being. Generally, holistic treatments do not suppress the symptoms that the body naturally produces, as do most medications prescribed by conventional doctors and vets. Holistic methods seek to cure disease by regaining balance and harmony in the patient's environment. Some of these methods include use of nutritional therapy, herbs, flower essences, aromatherapy, acupuncture, massage, chiropractic and, of course, the most popular holistic approach, homeopathy.

Homeopathy is a theory or system of treating illness with small doses of substances which, if administered in larger quantities, would produce the symptoms that the patient already has. This approach is often described as "like cures like." Although modern veterinary medicine is geared toward the "quick fix," homeopathy relies on the belief that, given the time, the body is able to heal itself and return to its natural, healthy state.

Choosing a remedy to cure a problem in our dogs is the difficult part of homeopathy. Consult with your vet for a professional diagnosis of your dog's symptoms. Often these symptoms require

immediate conventional care. If your vet is willing and knowledgeable, you may attempt a homeopathic remedy. Be aware that cortisone prevents homeopathic remedies from working. There are hundreds of possibilities and combinations to cure many problems in dogs, from basic physical problems such as excessive shedding, fleas or other parasites, unattractive doggy odor, bad breath, upset tummy, obesity,

dry, oily or dull coat, diarrhea, ear problems or eye discharge (including tears and dry or mucousy matter), to behavioral abnormalities such as fear of loud noises, habitual licking, poor appetite, excessive barking and various phobias. From alumina to zincum metallicum, the remedies span the planet and the imagination…from flowers and weeds to chemicals, insect droppings, diesel smoke and volcanic ash.

Using "Like to Treat Like"

Unlike conventional medicines that suppress symptoms, homeopathic remedies treat illnesses with small doses of substances that, if administered in larger quantities, would produce the symptoms that the patient already has. While the same homeopathic remedy can be used to treat different symptoms in different dogs, here are some interesting remedies and their uses.

Apis Mellifica
(made from honey bee venom) can be used for allergies or to reduce swelling that occurs in acutely infected kidneys.

Diesel Smoke
can be used to help control travel sickness.

Calcarea Fluorica
(made from calcium fluoride, which helps harden bone structure) can be useful in treating hard lumps in tissues.

Natrum Muriaticum
(made from common salt, sodium chloride) is useful in treating thin, thirsty dogs.

Nitricum Acidum
(made from nitric acid) is used for symptoms you would expect to see from contact with acids, such as lesions, especially where the skin joins the linings of body orifices or openings such as the lips and nostrils.

Symphytum
(made from the herb Knitbone, *Symphytum officianale*) is used to encourage bones to heal.

Urtica Urens
(made from the common stinging nettle) is used in treating painful, irritating rashes.

DALMATIAN

The term "old" is a qualitative term. For dogs, as well as their masters, old is relative. Certainly we can all distinguish between a puppy Dalmatian and an adult Dalmatian—there are the obvious physical traits, such as size, appearance and facial expressions, and personality traits. Puppies that are nasty are very rare. Puppies and young dogs like to play with children. Children's natural exuberance is a good match for the seemingly endless energy of young dogs. They like to run, jump, chase and retrieve. When dogs grow up and cease their interaction with children, they are often thought of as being too old to play with the kids. On the other hand, if a Dalmatian is only exposed to people over 60 years of age, its life will normally be less active and it will not seem to be getting old as its activity level slows down.

If people live to be 100 years old, dogs live to be 20 years old. While this is a good rule of thumb, it is very inaccurate. When trying to compare dog years to human years, you cannot make a generalization about all dogs. Dalmatians, for example, are considered to be seniors around the age of eight. With

proper care and attention, they can live well past their eighth year; the life expectancy for a healthy Dalmatian is between 12 and 15 years. Dogs are generally considered mature within three years, but they can reproduce even earlier. So the first three years of a dog's life are like seven times that of comparable humans. That means a 3-year-old dog is like a 21-year-old human. As the curve of comparison shows, there is no hard and fast rule for comparing dog and human ages. For example, many large breeds typically live for fewer years than

CDS: COGNITIVE DYSFUNCTION SYNDROME
"Old-Dog Syndrome"

There are many ways for you to evaluate old-dog syndrome. Veterinarians have defined CDS (cognitive dysfunction syndrome) as the gradual deterioration of cognitive abilities. These are indicated by changes in the dog's behavior. When a dog changes his routine response, and maladies have been eliminated as the cause of these behavioral changes, then CDS is the usual diagnosis.

More than half the dogs over eight years old suffer from some form of CDS. The older the dog, the more chance he has of suffering from CDS. In humans, doctors often dismiss the CDS behavioral changes as part of "winding down."

There are four major signs of CDS: frequent potty accidents inside the home, sleeping much more or much less than normal, acting confused and failing to respond to social stimuli.

SYMPTOMS OF CDS

FREQUENT POTTY ACCIDENTS
- *Urinates in the house.*
- *Defecates in the house.*
- *Doesn't signal that he wants to go out.*

SLEEP PATTERNS
- *Awakens more slowly.*
- *Sleeps more than normal during the day.*
- *Sleeps less during the night.*

CONFUSION
- *Goes outside and just stands there.*
- *Appears confused with a faraway look in his eyes.*
- *Hides more often.*
- *Doesn't recognize friends.*
- *Doesn't come when called.*
- *Walks around listlessly and without a destination.*

FAILURE TO RESPOND TO SOCIAL STIMULI
- *Comes to people less frequently, whether called or not.*
- *Doesn't tolerate petting for more than a short time.*
- *Doesn't come to the door when you return home.*

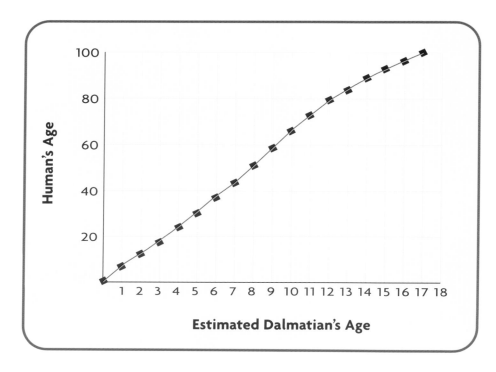

Estimated Dalmatian's Age

smaller ones. The comparison is made even more difficult, for not all humans age at the same rate...and human females live longer than human males.

WHAT TO LOOK FOR IN SENIORS
Most veterinarians and behaviorists use the Dalmatian's eight-year mark as the time to consider a dog a "senior." The term "senior" does not imply that the dog is geriatric and has begun to fail in mind and body. Aging is essentially a slowing process. Humans readily admit that they feel a difference in their activity level from age 20 to 30, and then from 30 to 40, etc. By treating the eight-year-old Dalmatian as a senior, owners are able to implement certain therapeutic and preventative medical strategies with the help of their veterinarians. A senior-care program should include at least two veterinary visits per year, screening sessions to determine the dog's health status, as well as nutritional counseling. Veterinarians determine the senior dog's health status through a blood smear for a complete blood count, serum chemistry profile with electrolytes, urinalysis,

WHEN YOUR DOG GETS OLD...
SIGNS THE OWNER CAN LOOK FOR

IF YOU NOTICE...	IT COULD INDICATE...
Discoloration of teeth and gums, foul breath, loss of appetite	Abcesses, gum disease, mouth lesions
Lumps, bumps, cysts, warts, fatty tumors	Cancers, benign or malignant
Cloudiness of eyes, apparent loss of sight.	Cataracts, lenticular sclerosis, PRA, retinal dysplasia, blindness
Flaky coat, alopecia (hair loss)	Hormonal problems, hypothyroidism
Obesity, appetite loss, excessive weight gain	Various problems
Household accidents, increased urination	Diabetes, kidney or bladder disease
Increased thirst	Kidney disease, diabetes mellitus
Change in sleeping habits, coughing	Heart disease
Difficulty moving	Arthritis, degenerative joint disease, spondylosis (degenerative spine disease)

IF YOU NOTICE ANY OF THESE SIGNS, AN APPOINTMENT SHOULD BE MADE IMMEDIATELY WITH A VETERINARIAN FOR A THOROUGH EVALUATION.

blood pressure check, electrocardiogram, ocular tonometry (pressure on the eyeball) and dental prophylaxis.

Such an extensive program for senior dogs is well advised before owners start to see the obvious physical signs of aging, such as slower and inhibited movement, graying, increased sleep/nap periods and disinterest in play and other activity. This preventative program promises a longer, healthier life for the aging dog. Among the physical

NOTICING THE SYMPTOMS

The symptoms listed below are symptoms that gradually appear and become more noticeable. They are not life-threatening; however, the symptoms below are to be taken very seriously and warrant a discussion with your veterinarian:

- Your dog cries and whimpers when he moves, and he stops running completely.
- Convulsions start or become more serious and frequent. The usual convulsion (spasm) is when the dog stiffens and starts to tremble, being unable or unwilling to move. The seizure usually lasts for 5 to 30 minutes.
- Your dog drinks more water and urinates more frequently. Wetting and bowel accidents take place indoors without warning.
- Vomiting becomes more and more frequent.

problems common in aging dogs are the loss of sight and hearing, arthritis, kidney and liver failure, diabetes mellitus, heart disease and Cushing's disease (a hormonal disease).

In addition to the physical manifestations discussed, there are some behavioral changes and problems related to aging dogs. Dogs suffering from hearing or vision loss, dental discomfort or arthritis can become aggressive. Likewise, the near-deaf and/or blind dog may be startled more easily and react in an unexpectedly aggressive manner. Seniors suffering from senility can become more impatient and irritable. Housesoiling accidents are associated with loss of mobility, kidney problem and loss of sphincter control as well as plaque accumulation, physiological brain changes and reactions to medications. Older dogs, just like young puppies, suffer from separation anxiety, which can lead to excessive barking, whining, housesoiling and destructive behavior. Seniors may become fearful of everyday sounds, such as vacuum cleaners, heaters, thunder and passing traffic. Some dogs have difficulty sleeping, due to discomfort, the need for frequent potty visits and the like.

Owners should avoid spoiling the older dog with too many treats. Obesity is a common problem in older dogs and subtracts years from their lives. Keep the senior dog as trim as possible, since excessive weight puts additional stress on the body's vital organs. Some breeders recommend supplementing the diet with foods high in fiber and lower in calories. Adding fresh vegetables to the senior's diet makes a tasty, low-calorie, low-fat supplement, but vegetables to avoid for the Dalmatian include asparagus, cauliflower, peas and other legumes, spinach and mushrooms. Vets also offer specialty diets for senior dogs that are worth exploring.

Your dog, as he nears his twilight years, needs his owner's

SIGNS OF AGING

An old dog starts to show one or more of the following symptoms:

- Sleep patterns are deeper and longer and the old dog is harder to awaken.

- Food intake diminishes.

- Responses to calls, whistles and other signals are ignored more and more.

- Eye contacts do not evoke tail wagging (assuming they once did).

- The hair on its face and paws starts to turn gray. The color breakdown usually starts around the eyes and mouth.

patience and good care more than ever. Never punish an older dog for an accident or abnormal behavior. For all the years of love, protection and companionship that your dog has provided, he deserves special attention and courtesies. The older dog may need to relieve himself at 3 a.m. because he can no longer hold it for eight hours. Older dogs may not be able to remain crated for more than two or three hours. It may be time to give up a spot on the couch or a chair to your old friend. Although he may not seem

Your older Dalmatian may continue to enjoy the same activities he has always enjoyed, just at a slower pace.

GETTING OLD

The bottom line is simply that a dog is getting old when you think he is getting old because he slows down in his general activities, including walking, running, eating, jumping and retrieving. On the other hand, certain activities increase, like more sleeping, more barking and more repetition of habits like going to the door when you put your coat on without being called.

as enthusiastic about your attention and petting, he does appreciate the considerations you offer as he gets older.

Your Dalmatian does not understand why his world is slowing down. Owners must make the transition into the golden years as pleasant and rewarding as possible.

WHEN THE TIME COMES

You are never fully prepared to make a rational decision about putting your dog to sleep. It is very obvious that you love your Dalmatian or you would not be reading this book. Putting a loved dog to sleep is extremely difficult. It is a decision that must be made with your veterinarian. You are usually forced to make the decision when your dog experiences one or more life-threatening symptoms, requiring you to seek veterinary help.

If the prognosis of the malady indicates the end is near and your beloved pet will only suffer more and experience no enjoyment for the balance of his life, then euthanasia is the right choice.

WHAT IS EUTHANASIA?

Euthanasia derives from the Greek, meaning *good death.* In other words, it means the planned, painless killing of a dog suffering from a painful, incurable condition, or who is so aged that he cannot walk, see, eat or control his excretory functions.

Euthanasia is usually accomplished by injection with an overdose of an anesthesia or barbiturate. Aside from the prick of the needle, the experience is usually painless.

MAKING THE DECISION

The decision to euthanize your dog is never easy. The days during which the dog becomes ill and the end occurs can be unusually stressful for you. If this is your first experience with the death of a loved one, you may need the comfort dictated by your religious beliefs. If you are the head of the family and have children, you should have involved them in the decision of putting your Dalmatian to sleep. Usually your dog can be maintained on drugs for a few days in order to give you ample time to make a decision. During this time, talking with members of your family or even people who have lived through this same experience can ease the burden of your inevitable decision.

THE FINAL RESTING PLACE

Dogs can have some of the same privileges as humans. They can be buried in a pet cemetery, which is generally expensive, or can be buried in your yard in a place suitably marked with some stone or newly planted tree or bush. Alternatively, they can be cremated and the ashes returned to you, or some people prefer to leave their dogs at the clinic for the vet to dispose of.

All of these options should be

> **EUTHANASIA SERVICES**
> Euthanasia must be done by a licensed vet, who may be considerate enough to come to your home. There also may be societies for the prevention of cruelty to animals in your area. They often offer this service upon a vet's recommendation.

discussed frankly and openly with your veterinarian. Do not be afraid to ask financial questions. Cremations can be individual, but a less expensive option is mass cremation, although of course the ashes cannot then be returned. If you want a private cremation,

There are pet cemeteries in which you can lay your dog to rest. Your veterinarian will usually be able to help you locate one.

Cemeteries for pets usually have places for funeral urns that contain your pet's ashes.

there are crematoriums where this can be arranged. Vets can usually arrange cremation services on your behalf.

GETTING ANOTHER DOG?

The grief of losing your beloved dog will be as lasting as the grief of losing a human friend or relative. In most cases, if your dog died of old age (if there is such a thing), he had slowed down considerably. Do you want a new Dalmatian puppy to replace him? Or are you better off finding a more mature Dalmatian, say two to three years of age, which will

Special gravestones and markers often indicate pets' graves; some graves may even be decorated with flowers or favorite toys.

usually be housebroken and will have an already developed personality. In this case, you can find out if you like each other after a few hours of being together.

The decision is, of course, your own. Do you want another Dalmatian or perhaps a different breed so as to avoid comparison with your beloved friend? Most people usually buy the same breed because they know (and love) the characteristics of that breed. Then, too, they often know people who have the same breed and perhaps they are lucky enough that a breeder they know and respect expects a litter soon. What could be better?

SHOWING YOUR
DALMATIAN

To the novice, exhibiting a Dalmatian in the show ring may look easy, but it takes a lot of hard work and devotion to do top winning at a show such as the prestigious Westminster Kennel Club dog show, not to mention a little luck too!

An important concept that you must understand is that the dogs are not actually compared against one another. The judge compares each dog against his breed standard, which is the AKC-approved written description of the ideal specimen of the breed. Breeders attempt to get as close to this ideal as possible with every litter, but theoretically the "perfect" dog is so elusive that it is impossible. If you are interested in exploring the world of dog showing, your best bet is to join your local breed club or the national parent club, which is the Dalmatian Club of America (DCA). These clubs often host both regional and national specialties, shows only for Dalmatians, which can include conformation as well as obedience, road and agility trials. Even if you have no intention of competing, a specialty is like a festival for lovers of the breed who congregate to share their favorite topic: Dals! Clubs also send out newsletters, and some organize training days and seminars in order that people may learn more

about their chosen breed. To locate the breed club closest to you, contact the DCA or the AKC.

In the US, the AKC offers three kinds of conformation shows: an all-breed show (for all AKC-recognized breeds); a specialty show (for one breed only, usually sponsored by the parent club) and a Group show (for all breeds in the Group).

For a dog to become an AKC champion of record, the dog must accumulate 15 points at the shows from at least three different judges, including two "majors." A "major" is defined as a three-, four- or five-point win, and the number of points per win is determined on the number of dogs entered in the show on the day. Depending on the breed, the number of points that are awarded varies. In a breed as popular as the Dalmatian, more dogs are needed to rack up the

Dog showing can be a fun and rewarding activity for owners to try. Most of the attendees are dog lovers just like you!

Is there a greater joy than working hard to train your Dalmatian and then having him win a few prizes?

CLUB CONTACTS

You can get information about dog shows from the national kennel clubs:

American Kennel Club
5580 Centerview Dr., Raleigh, NC 27606-3390
www.akc.org

United Kennel Club
100 E. Kilgore Road, Kalamazoo, MI 49002
www.ukcdogs.com

Canadian Kennel Club
89 Skyway Ave., Suite 100, Etobicoke, Ontario
M9W 6R4, Canada
www.ckc.ca

The Kennel Club
1-5 Clarges St., Piccadilly,
London W1Y 8AB, UK
www.the-kennel-club.org.uk

points. At any dog show, only one dog and one bitch of each breed can win points.

Dogs and bitches never compete against each other in the classes. Non-champion dogs are called "class dogs" because they compete in one of five classes. Dogs are entered in a particular class depending on their age and previous show wins. To begin, there is the Puppy Class; this class is followed by the Novice Class (for dogs that have not won any first prizes except in the Puppy Class or three first prizes in the Novice Class and have not accumulated any points toward their champion title); the Bred-by Exhibitor Class; the American-bred Class; and the Open Class (for any dog that is not a champion).

The judge at the show begins judging the Puppy Class, first dogs and then bitches, and proceeds through the classes. The judge places his winners first through fourth in each class. In the Winners Class, the first-place winners of each class compete with one another to determine Winners Dog and Winners Bitch. The judge also places a Reserve Winners Dog and Reserve Winners Bitch, which could be awarded the points in the case of a disqualification. The Winners Dog and Winners Bitch, the two that are awarded the points for the breed, then compete with any champions of record entered in the show. The judge reviews the Winners Dog, Winners Bitch and all of the champions to select his Best of Breed. The Best of Winners is selected between the Winners Dog and Winners Bitch. Were one of these two to be selected Best of

an all-breed show compete for Best in Show.

If your Dalmatian is six months of age or older and registered with the AKC, you can enter him in a dog

Handlers stand with their Dalmatians in the ring and await the judge's inspection.

Breed, he or she would automatically be named Best of Winners as well. Finally the judge selects his Best of Opposite Sex to the Best of Breed winner.

At a Group show or all-breed show, the Best of Breed winners from each breed then compete against one another for Group One through Group Four. The judge compares each Best of Breed to his breed standard, and the dog that most closely lives up to the ideal for his breed is selected as Group One. Finally, all seven group winners at

show where the breed is offered classes. Provided that your Dalmatian does not have a disqualifying fault, he can compete. Only unaltered dogs can be entered in a

AKC GROUPS

For showing purposes, the American Kennel Club divides its recognized breeds into seven groups: Sporting Dogs, Hounds, Working Dogs, Terriers, Toys, Non-Sporting Dogs and Herding Dogs.

In both agility and obedience competition, dogs are required to clear a number of jumps.

BECOMING A CHAMPION

An official AKC champion of record requires that a dog accumulate 15 points under three different judges, including two "majors" under different judges. Points are awarded based on the number of dogs entered into competition, varying from breed to breed and place to place. A win of three, four or five points is considered a "major." The AKC annually assigns a schedule of points to adjust to the variations that accompany a breed's popularity and the population of a given area.

dog show, so if you have spayed or neutered your Dalmatian, you cannot compete in conformation shows. The reason for this is simple. Dog shows are the main forum to prove which representatives in a breed are worthy of being bred. Only dogs that have achieved championships—the AKC "seal of approval" for quality in pure-bred dogs—should be bred. Altered dogs, however, can participate in other AKC events such as obedience trials and the Canine Good Citizen® program.

If you are not in the top four in your class at your first show, do not be discouraged. Remember that the winners were once in your shoes and have devoted many hours and much money to earn the placement. If you're not successful in conformation, it may be time to consider a different dog sport or to just enjoy your Dalmatian as a pet. Parent clubs offer other events, such as agility, tracking, obedience, road trials and more.

OBEDIENCE TRIALS
Obedience trials in the US trace back to the early 1930s; today there are over 2,000 trials held in the US every year, with more than 100,000 dogs competing. Any registered AKC dog can enter an obedience trial, regard-

Colorful medals, ribbons and trophies are often awarded to the winners at dog shows.

less of conformational disqualifications or neutering.

Obedience trials are divided into three levels of progressive difficulty, each consisting of a set of exercises. At the first level, the Novice, dogs compete for the title Companion Dog (CD); at the intermediate level, the Open, dogs compete for the title Companion Dog Excellent (CDX); and at the advanced level, the Utility, dogs compete for the title Utility Dog (UD). Classes are sub-divided into "A" (for beginners) and "B" (for more experienced handlers). A perfect score at any level is 200, and a dog must score 170 or better to earn a "leg," of which three are needed to earn the title. To earn points, the dog must score more than 50% of the available points in each exercise; the possible points range from 20 to 40.

Once a dog has earned the UD title, he can compete with other proven obedience dogs for the

---

MEET THE AKC
The AKC is the main governing body of the dog sport in the United States. Founded in 1884, the AKC consists of 500 or more independent dog clubs plus 4,500 affiliate clubs, all of which follow the AKC rules and regulations. Additionally, the AKC maintains a registry for pure-bred dogs in the US and works to preserve the integrity of the sport and its continuation in the country. Over 1,000,000 dogs are registered each year, representing about 150 recognized breeds. There are over 15,000 competitive events held annually for which over 2,000,000 dogs enter to participate. Dogs compete to earn over 40 different titles, from Champion to Companion Dog to Master Agility Champion.

coveted title of Utility Dog Excellent (UDX). Utility Dogs who earn "legs" in Open B and Utility B earn points toward their Obedience Trial Champion (OTCh.) title, established by the AKC in 1997. To become an OTCh., a dog needs to earn 100 points, which requires three first places in Open B and Utility under three different judges.

The Grand Prix of obedience trials, the AKC National Obedience Invitational gives qualifying Utility Dogs the chance to win the newest and highest title: National Obedience Champion (NOC). Only the top 25 ranked obedience dogs, plus any dog ranked in the top 3 in his breed, are allowed to compete.

AGILITY TRIALS
Having had its origins in the UK back in 1977, AKC agility had its official

> **NO SHOW**
> Never show a dog that is sick or recovering from surgery or infection. Not only will this put your own dog under a tremendous amount of stress, but you will also put other dogs at risk of contracting any illness your dog has. Likewise, bitches who are in heat will distract and disrupt the performances of males who are competing, and bitches that are pregnant will likely be stressed and exhausted by a long day of showing.

beginning in the US in August 1994, when the first licensed agility trials were held. The AKC allows all registered breeds (including Miscellaneous Class breeds) to participate, providing the dog is 12 months of age or older. Agility is designed so that the handler demonstrates how well the dog can work at his side. The handler directs his dog over an obstacle course that includes jumps, tires, the dog walk, weave poles, pipe tunnels, collapsed tunnels, etc. While working his way through the course, the dog must keep one eye and ear on the handler and the rest of his body on the course. The handler gives verbal and hand signals to guide the dog through the course.

The first organization to promote agility trials in the US was the United States Dog Agility Association, Inc. (USDAA). Both the USDAA and the AKC offer titles to winning dogs. Three titles are

Although Dals don't participate in field trials for retrievers, they do derive from hunting dogs and can be trained to work on water on land.

available through the USDAA: Agility Dog (AD), Advanced Agility Dog (AAD) and Master Agility Dog (MAD). The AKC offers Novice Agility (NA), Open Agility (OA), Agility Excellent (AX) and Master Agility Excellent (MX). Beyond these four AKC titles, dogs can win additional ones in "jumper" classes, Jumpers with Weave

One of the things that the judge will evaluate is your Dalmatian's gait.

Novice (NAJ), Open (OAJ) and Excellent (MXJ), which lead to the ultimate title(s): MACH, Master Agility Champion. Dogs can continue to add number designations to the MACH titles, indicating how many times the dog has met the MACH requirements, such as MACH1, MACH2, etc.

TRACKING
Any dog is capable of tracking, using his nose to follow a trail. The AKC started tracking tests in 1937. Ten years later, in 1947, the AKC offered the first title, Tracking Dog (TD). It was not until 1980 that the AKC added the Tracking Dog Excellent title (TDX), which was followed by the Versatile Surface Tracking title (VST) in 1995. The title Champion

CANINE GOOD CITIZEN®
PROGRAM

Have you ever considered getting your dog "certified"? The AKC's Canine Good Citizen® Program affords your dog just that opportunity. Your dog shows that he is a well-behaved canine citizen, using the basic training and good manners you have taught him, by taking a series of ten tests that illustrate that he can behave properly at home, in a public place and around other dogs. The tests are administered by participating dog clubs, colleges, 4-H clubs, scouts and other community groups and are open to all pure-bred and mixed-breed dogs. Upon passing the ten tests, the suffix CGC is then applied to your dog's name.

The ten tests are: 1. Accepting a friendly stranger; 2. Sitting politely for petting; 3. Appearance and grooming; 4. Walking on a lead; 5. Walking through a group of people; 6. Sit, down and stay on command; 7. Coming when called; 8. Meeting another dog; 9. Calm reaction to distractions; 10. Separation from owner.

JUNIOR SHOWMANSHIP

For budding dog handlers, ages 10 to 18 years, Junior Showmanship competitions are an excellent training ground for the next generation of dog professionals. Owning and caring for a dog are wonderful methods of teaching children responsibility, and Junior Showmanship builds upon that foundation. Juniors learn by grooming, handling and training their dogs, and the quality of junior's presentation of the dog (and himself) is evaluated by a licensed judge. The junior can enter with any registered AKC dog to compete, including an ILP, provided that the dog lives with him or a member of his family.

Junior Showmanship competitions are divided into two classes: Novice (for beginners) and Open (for juniors show have three first place wins in the Novice Class). The junior must run with the dog with the rest of the handlers and dogs, stack the dog for examination and individually gait the dog in a specific pattern. Juniors should practice with a handling class or an experienced handler before entering the Novice Class so that they recognize all the jargon that the judge may use.

A National Junior Organization was founded in 1997 to help promote the sport of dog showing among young people. The AKC also offers a Junior Scholarship for juniors who excel in the program.

Tracker (CT) is awarded to a dog who has earned all three titles.

In the beginning level of tracking, the owner follows the dog through a field on a long lead. To earn the TD title, the dog must follow a track laid by a human 30 to 120 minutes prior. The track is about 500 yards with up to 5 directional changes. The TDX requires that the dog follow a track that is 3 to 5 hours old over a course up to 1,000 yards with up to 7 directional changes. The VST requires that the dog follow a track up to 5 hours old through an urban setting.

ROAD TRIALS

Road trials, which are organized competitions designed to test the Dalmatian's coaching abilities, have been held in America since 1906. They are popular with many fanciers, as they enable their dogs to do the work for which Dals were intended, that of accompanying their owners on journeys and protecting the coach, horse and owner.

There are three types of tests and titles in a road trial: the Coaching Certificate (CC) test, which consists of exercises to evaluate a dog's coaching ability; the Road Dog (RD) test, in which the coaching exercises are completed along with a 12.5-mile distance to test endurance; and the Road Dog Excellent (RDX) test, which consists of the coaching exercises along with a 25-mile distance. The dogs must perform the exercises with accuracy and complete the given distances in a certain time frame, while at the same time display proper behavior and enthusiasm toward the work being done. In addition to being judged and scored on the exercises, dogs entered in the RD and RDX tests must pass veterinary examinations before, during and after the completing the given distances.

Obviously, road trials require a considerable amount of space; they have been held in conjunction with the DCA's National Specialty when the location has been suitable. The Dalmatian Club of America publishes an extensive set of road trial rules and regulations, which can be obtained on the DCA's website or by contacting the club.

Bringing home a ribbon... a successful day in the show ring.

INDEX

*Page numbers in **boldface** indicate illustrations.*

My Dalmatian

PUT YOUR PUPPY'S FIRST PICTURE HERE

Dog's Name _____

Date _____ Photographer _____